22 000 MILES

A Father and Son's Cycling Adventures

Richard Seipp

little peak press

**To Ann, without whom none of
this would have been possible.**

22 000 Miles – Richard Seipp

First published in 2020 by Little Peak Press

www.littlepeak.co.uk

Copyright © Richard Seipp 2020

Richard Seipp has asserted his rights under the Copyright, Designs and Patents Act 1998 to be identified as the author of this work.

This book is a work of non-fiction based on the life, experiences and recollections of Richard Seipp. In some limited cases the names of people, places, dates and sequences or the details of events have been changed solely to protect the privacy of others. The author has stated to the publishers that, except in such minor respects not affecting the substantial accuracy of the work, the contents of the book are true.

Edited by Jo Allen & Heather Dawe

Unless otherwise stated, all photography by Richard Seipp

Design and Production by Rhiannon Hughes,
www.theyorkshirewordwright.co.uk

A CIP catalogue record for this book is available from the British Library.

ISBN: 978-1-9160812-2-2

FSC
www.fsc.org
MIX
Paper from
responsible sources
FSC® C005094

Printed and bound in the UK

CONTENTS

FOREWORD

I stood by the fire watching the flames dance in that hypnotic way they do, the smell of woodsmoke, sound of music and laughter surrounding me. I'm at 'The Big Shakeout', a festival run by one of my sponsors that pulls together a crowd of like-minded enthusiasts to celebrate their love of the outdoors. It's late in the evening and I'm enjoying myself with friends new and old. In the dim light, I see someone approaching I recognise. A person I feel as though I've been friends with for a lifetime, but have rarely met. I guess this is the power of social media these days. He walks up, shakes my hand, and says 'hello mate'. That man is Rich Seipp.

I'd heard Rich's name a few years earlier, probably off the back of a conversation about tandems. When people know you ride a tandem, as I do, it shows how small the world is out there – the same names pop into conversation time and time again – maybe it's because of our love for adventure and the outdoors and we just happen to both ride a tandem. I was told that Rich and his young son Tom rode theirs to some interesting places and I should check them out, which, of course, out of interest I did.

It appeared we did have a lot in common; this father and son tandem combination were having grand adventures of their own all over the country. It's never long before you get to know someone well enough to know that nothing surprises you anymore. I watched from afar, unsurprised, as each new challenge was set and quickly achieved. The ironic thing was I didn't actually know them at all. Over the next couple of years I followed their exploits on social media, unfortunately missing them at the few events I attended, but always keeping in touch via messages, normally to congratulate them on their achievements. I watched Tom quickly outgrow the tandem and start riding his solo bike, taking on long, serious endurance races, one after another, the kind of races grown men and women don't always finish. In years to come, they'll call Tom a 'talented bike rider', massively overlooking all the experiences he has been through on his bike at a young age.

11

Experiences the classroom cannot teach, and this will be put down to 'talent'. They will say 'it's in his blood, he's one of the lucky ones'.

That particular evening, standing by the fire with a beer, Rich and I talk like old friends. Sharing tales of adventures both past and planned, laughing about misadventures and the lessons learned along the way. I ask Rich how Tom is doing, and he looks up and gestures over my shoulder. Behind me is a large marquee, colourful spinning disco lighting illuminating its white canvas walls, while Queen's 'Bohemian Rhapsody' spills from its rolled-up open sides. I see Tom, head flung back as he sings at the top of his voice, dancing with all his might, entertaining the crowd around him. I turn back to Rich and smile, impressed by Tom's enthusiasm at this late hour. Rich tells me they are planning to do the Tour Divide the following year; it's the holy grail of bikepacking and a route I'd love to ride. I'm excited for them both, but envious too. Two thousand, seven hundred miles long, running from Canada to Mexico... later that evening I drift off to sleep in my tiny dew-covered tent, dreaming of that massive adventure.

When I received an email from Rich saying he'd written a book, I was instantly excited, and reading on, incredibly humbled when he had asked me to write this foreword. I couldn't wait to read about their adventures together. I wondered what stories he'd include and would he leave anything out? It can't have been easy choosing when you have a back catalogue of adventures like these two. A few weeks later a copy appeared for me to read. I let it sit there for a couple of days, before I turned the first few pages.

As I read though these chapters, I was captivated with Rich's writing, uncomplicated and honest, yet full of experiences and learning. He takes you on a wonderful journey through their adventures, each gaining in distance and commitment, and putting into practice what the two of them had learnt from the last one. He reveals Tom's willingness to take on these challenges at such a young age, full-heartedly supported by Rich, his wife Ann and sister Skye. Not all their rides worked out as they had planned, yet together they show the value of overcoming adversity to achieve the desired outcome. Rich weaves this story about growth through the chapters which I loved. How a young father learns to share his passion with his growing daughter and son, his own time on the bike becoming their time, while Tom grows with every ride, gaining the strength and skillset to make him one of the most experienced bikepackers in the country at the ripe old age of fifteen.

22 000 Miles is an inspiring book for the seasoned bikepacker, the adventure newbie and the families wanting to explore more by bike. I really hope you enjoy reading about their journey as I did.

Ride safe

Steve Bate MBE
Double Paralympic and World Champion Cyclist.

CHAPTER 1
Adult Portions

I rode bikes before my wife Ann and I had our children, Skye and Tom. When I was a boy, it was transportation to school and a cheap way of getting out of Leeds at the weekend. The only time I went out with a group was on a school-organised ride and I remember being disheartened because I couldn't keep up with quicker riders. I kept on riding though. I enjoyed cycling, but knew nothing of the races and how important they were to many riders. The Tour de France was not on my radar. I didn't have cycling heroes. Cycling was what I made of it. When I started work my commute was by bike. The only racing I did was chasing the bus into town. At weekends I'd ride into the Yorkshire countryside seeking new roads and places to visit.

In the 1980s, when mountain bikes arrived in the UK, I traded my second-hand road bike for a Specialized Rockhopper. I dabbled with racing mountain bikes – mostly 24-hour solo events. I was never that close to getting on to the podium, partly because I never really did any training. I remember back in the day, you needed to send in a resumé of sorts to get a place to ride solo in one of the big 24-hour races like Mountain Mayhem or Sleepless in the Saddle. This made sense, as riding a bike round laps of a circuit for 24 hours without sleep is an unusual thing to do.

Finishing a 24-hour race used to be my goal. Fell running, climbing, hill walking, caving and canoeing – over the years all had their time, but I always came back to cycling. A bit of a dabbler – most certainly not an obsessive cyclist. Definitely a big fan of the outdoors though.

When our first child – our daughter Skye – arrived, cycling took a back seat for a while. Ann and I had never planned on having kids, but I soon discovered that looking after Skye was wonderful. Riding my bike could wait until she was a bit older. After a year or so, we bought a trailer for her to travel in.

We'd ride out for an hour on forest tracks or other traffic-free routes, heading for a café to drink hot chocolate and eat cake. Nothing epic about these rides except maybe, if we were lucky, the size of the slice of cake. The emphasis was always on having a good time outside. When Skye got older she came out riding with me, first on a tagalong bike and later on her own bike.

Tom is three years Skye's junior and he started learning to ride his bike when he was four. Once he was off stabilisers, we'd head down the disused railway track from our village towards the next village three miles away.

Tom's first ride.

He'd fall off if he wasn't paying attention. He'd cry, like little kids do, but he'd always pick up his bike, get back on and give it another go. Though still so young, it was obvious he had a certain resilience. I wasn't bothered one way or the other if my kids wanted to ride bikes with me as cycling had always been 'me time'. I was impressed though with both kids' efforts, and more than happy to encourage them.

On my road bike I'd average over 15mph – riding with kids was so slow in comparison. We'd go out for a few hours and cover less than ten miles. I learned quickly that I needed plenty of warm clothes and patience. There were times of frustration, but slowly my attitude changed. Riding was no longer about just what I wanted to do – it was now a thing that we did as a family.

I recall an outing when Tom was five years old which showed he wanted to ride just that little bit further. It was the summer holidays, and the weather forecast was for sunshine. I suggested to Tom and Skye that we take the bikes to the Tissington trail, a disused railway line in the Peak District near home. I promised them café stops and ice creams. We parked the car near the start of the trail around midday and set off south with no other plan than to have fun. After only three and a half miles we stopped for our first lot of refreshments at the Parsley Hay café. I asked the kids if they fancied riding a little further, to which they replied 'yes'. The next ten miles passed without any grumbles. At Tissington we had an ice cream and a drink. I felt they'd done well to ride 14 and a half miles and had planned to turn back at that point, but Tom asked how much further it would be to the end of the trail at Ashbourne. The answer was another three and a half miles and Skye was happy to ride a little further. So we went on to Ashbourne and searched out a café where I ordered beans on toast for three. Asked if that would be one adult and two kids' portions, I confessed it would be three adult portions. The kids had no problem clearing their plates and even ordered puddings. Refuelled, all that was left for the rest of the day was to ride the 18 miles back to the car.

As you leave Ashbourne on the Tissington trail there's quite a bit of uphill. It was clear that both Tom and Skye were a bit tired. I assisted them by giving them a little push or giving them a slingshot as riders do when racing the Madison at the velodrome. We got back to the car at 8pm when Ann called to ask where we were as we were meant to be at my in-laws for supper. I said we'd be there shortly. As I drove back to Hayfield the kids fell asleep. Not surprising, considering they'd ridden 36 miles. Getting home around 10pm, Tom asked: "Can we go for a bike ride again tomorrow?" He was obviously hooked and though clearly tired, he wanted to do it all again. In the future I'd have to get used to not riding solo, but adjusting my riding to his.

Our first big bike ride had been a success. I'd left it to the kids to decide how far they wanted to ride. There'd been no pressure to go far, it just turned out that way. The sun was shining and there was food and drink aplenty. I'd given them space and guidance, but left them to make their own decisions. I certainly wouldn't have suggested that we might have ridden all the way to Ashbourne and back. Skye enjoyed the day and rode really well, but her talents took her in a different direction. A spark was lit for Tom that day that has shaped not just his life, but mine as well.

CHAPTER 2
Festive 500

It was Christmas Eve 2012 and Tom was seven years old. Instead of being wrapped up toasty in front of the fire at home, eagerly waiting to unwrap his presents on Christmas Day, he was riding his bike in Derbyshire, back along the Tissington trail. We'd cycled there together and were 37 kilometres from home. Leaving at first light, we'd had a great morning. Spirits had been high and there were lots of smiles. But after starting off dry and cool, the weather slowly changed to wet and freezing with flurries of sleety snow. And then Tom got cold. He was crying, and not because there would be nothing for him in Santa's sack the following morning...

Let me go back in time and introduce James. James is a friend, another cyclist. He often visits, and the conversation invariably gets round to cycling exploits, past or forthcoming, and he'd mentioned a challenge called the 'Rapha Festive 500'. The '500' are kilometres and the goal is to ride that distance between Christmas Eve and New Year's Eve, a total of eight days. James was considering the challenge and asked if I was up for it. I said yes, though in a 'maybe I will, yet probably I won't' kind of way. Christmas Eve wouldn't be a problem, but riding on Christmas Day and Boxing Day would be a definite 'maybe'. Tom was listening intently to James though.

"So, Dad, can we do the Festive 500?"

My initial response was a knee-jerk 'no', but Tom was not easily dissuaded. He did some quick maths: 500 divided by 8 equals 63 kilometres or just under 40 miles a day and stated, correctly, that he'd ridden over 40 miles a day on more than one occasion, so why not? I said we'd be short on daylight and I didn't like the idea of him riding on wintry roads. His response was that we'd get up early, buy more lights to make us easier to be seen, and ride some of the miles on the disused railway lines near Buxton. Seven years old with reasoning beyond his age. What can you say?

My father used words like 'can't' and phrases like 'because I say so'. No discussions; no apparent logic. I am not that sort of parent. If Tom thought he could do the ride, why shouldn't he? We'd give it a go. Though, to be honest, I didn't think we'd make it to the end. Forty miles in a day in good weather and daylight is one thing. However, that distance every day for eight days back-to-back during a British winter is a test for many adults who are regular cyclists, never mind a child.

Having thought it through and decided we'd do it, I'd checked the weather forecast the night before we started – the temperature would be above freezing with little chance of rain. Our plan was to get some extra miles done on the first day just in case there was bad weather later in the week. However, setting off just after first light, it soon became apparent the weather wasn't going to play nice after all. I guess if it had started raining right from the start we'd have turned around and gone straight back home. But I was tempted into thinking it would get better, at least until where I began this story 37 kilometres into our planned ride along the old railway line that forms the Tissington trail running from near Parsley Hay to just south of Buxton.

They say there's no such thing as the wrong weather for cycling, only the wrong clothes. On this particular occasion we got the ideal balance of clothing and weather slightly, but worryingly, wrong. Tom had layers of warm clothes under his waterproofs, a woolly hat and overshoes, but there was a chink in his armour – his usually toasty fleece gloves were not waterproof and his hands were icy cold. Tom had changed from his usual smiley self to being really not happy. I curse my stupidity for this oversight. As we neared the visitor centre at Parsley Hey, the rain turned to sleet. We could head back home, but I was hoping the café might be open so he could warm up.

The summertime café was closed, of course, but thankfully the toilets alongside were open and had a hot air hand drier. Tom dried his hands, dried his gloves, and cheered up considerably. Mindful that the weather was definitely not improving, I realised simply turning round and heading home might not be the best plan – we needed an escape route. With Tom dry and happy we headed out again, my plan being to ride quickly to Buxton some eight miles away and get a train home. But the sleet was still falling so Tom's hands were soon wet and, even worse, I could see he was getting cold again and becoming withdrawn – the warning signs of hypothermia. We needed to be somewhere warm and dry quickly. As we hit the outskirts of Buxton I spotted a café. Once inside, Tom became happier but was still shivering. The café supplied sausage sandwiches and big mugs of hot chocolate and in front of the fire he was soon warm inside and out.

While he recovered and chatted to a fellow cyclist about how rubbish his gloves were, I phoned Ann to see if she could collect us. She was miles away in Manchester shopping with Skye for last-minute Christmas things, but a call to my father-in-law was more fruitful. Within the hour we'd been rescued and were imbibing more hot chocolate in front of another roaring fire. I felt a mixture of relief that things hadn't turned out worse, and stupidity that we'd been in that situation in the first place.

Back at home I didn't even bother to mention the Festive 500. I couldn't imagine after the day that Tom had experienced that he'd want to ride his bike anytime soon, if ever again. That weighed heavily on my mind. Lots of people tell their tales about going into the great outdoors unprepared, and never wishing to repeat the experience. Had I unintentionally sown that seed? I was annoyed with my oversight. I overheard Tom chatting to his mum about waterproof gloves, confusingly, as he didn't then own any. I'd had enough of bike talk for one day, and instead settled on the settee with a glass of wine and some seasonal telly.

If you have kids, you'll know that early on Christmas Day, by the time you wake up, your kids will have already been busy doing things for hours. Opening presents and playing with them, still in pyjamas. I woke up with Tom gazing at me. He didn't have a toy. Instead, he held a cup of freshly ground percolated coffee he'd made for me. His first words weren't 'here's your coffee', or 'Happy Christmas', but 'get out of bed, we're off out on our bikes'.

"Come on," he said "we can do some more miles before we go to Granny's for Christmas dinner."

I had no words. I was confused. Then I realised he was on about continuing the Festive 500. After the previous day's experience I was amazed, but quickly took stock. "You haven't any suitable gloves," I said, "I don't want a repeat of yesterday." But he'd thought that through. "Don't worry," he said, "Mummy found me some waterproof gloves to go over my fleecy gloves and keep my hands warm." The 'waterproof gloves' are bright yellow washing-up gloves! There are no excuses then, are there?

I gulp down the coffee, throw on my cycling clothes, and we ride. Quiet roads took us over the hill to Glossop and from there to Holme Moss – this is the first time Tom has climbed this hill, which figured in the Tour de France when it visited Yorkshire. At the top of the hill we stopped for a quick photo and something to eat – 'something' being mince pies made by Ann. I ate mine, but Tom wasn't bothered about his after the first bite so I tried to flick what was left of it out of his hand. Unfortunately, this went straight into his eye. Day two and Tom was crying again, though admittedly only suffering in one eye instead of two hands. An improvement, eh? Despite only having half his vision, he descended the other side of the hill towards Holmfirth quickly. Thankfully his eye soon settled down and we carried on riding towards our Christmas dinner with Granny in Leeds.

Day three and we had work to do. We needed a big day on the bikes. Fortunately the weather was a bit more welcoming. We headed south in the direction of Cheshire on a fairly flat route that yielded a good distance. The Middlewood Way, along another disused railway line, took us towards Macclesfield. We stopped there to refuel with jelly babies and bask in the winter sun before continuing south as far as Congleton where we turned to head back.

At Jodrell Bank the café was disappointingly shut, so no hot drinks that day. What we did get instead was a fair number of hawthorn punctures. Luckily we'd brought four spare tubes. Our day didn't improve as dusk fell and the weather turned, so we were grateful for our waterproofs. It was dark when we arrived home after 8 hours and 95 kilometres – but we were back on track to complete the Festive 500.

Day four dawned and we were already 200 kilometres into our challenge, so we'd planned a ride along a nearby canal to a coffee shop for hot chocolate and cake. Carelessly I'd done a rubbish job of removing the thorns after the previous day's puncture-fest and we punctured three tyres before we'd even started. I took more care this time, but we set out later than planned. Other than crossing roads our route was traffic-free, so it should have been a stress-free day. Unhelpfully, British Waterways had been back out trimming hedges, and our progress was again slowed by punctures. I was getting grumpy, though the coffee shop cheered me up. Reversing our route we had an incident-free ride back home.

On day five we revisited the Tissington trail. The weather was, as forecast, grim. I was grateful we didn't need to share space with any other traffic in the poor visibility. Wrapped up warm and prepared for the conditions, rain and wind were our almost permanent companions.

We arrived in Ashbourne and found a café where the owner looked horrified at our mud-splattered appearance though he didn't turn us away, which was the important thing. A sausage and egg sandwich each followed by chocolate cake and we were good to go. On a warm summer's day this trail would be busy with cyclists and walkers. On that wet December day we saw hardly anyone and savoured the quietness. Getting home after 83km, despite the wild, wet weather, Tom was eagerly talking about what we'd do the next day.

We'd arranged to meet our friend Amy at Ashbourne on day six, again choosing the Tissington trail. After lunch with her we all rode back towards Parsley Hey. It was raining, though by now we were accustomed to it. On day seven we ventured a bit further afield. We got a lift into Manchester then followed the Rochdale canal to Todmorden to watch some friends competing in a cyclo-cross race. Tom was confused by people coming up to congratulate him, not realising that word had spread about what he'd achieved over the previous few days.

New Year's Eve was the final day of our challenge and we had 57km to ride. There hadn't been a dry day yet on the Festive 500 and this last was no different. I didn't realise until we were a few miles from home that I'd not worn my waterproof jacket – unsurprisingly I was quite wet. We rode over the Snake Pass to the Woodbine café in Hope where we ate cake and Tom was kindly given a free hot chocolate by the café's owner as reward for his efforts.

Once home we uploaded our GPS data to Strava. I'd told him we would be out for a long time and so it proved. Tom had finished his first Festive 500, having ridden 504km in 34 hours over 8 days and become the youngest rider to complete the challenge.

I was proud and am still proud of his achievement. He decided he wanted to reach that goal, and he did. The opportunities for him to throw in the towel were many. Having had early stage hypothermia myself in the past as he did on that first day, I can say that for him to want to get out on his bike the next day was quite amazing.

Since the very first of our cycling trips together we've had an unwritten rule which is if we are going to go for a ride, then it is with 100% commitment. However, if one of us doesn't want to go for a ride, that's fine. Don't be a messer. That Christmas I guess Tom had committed to the Festive 500. That was that. And if Tom is committed, then it's only fair that I should be too.

We both learned lessons over those days riding the Festive 500. Lessons that enabled us both to see that boundaries are quite often self-imposed. How far can you ride? How far can your child ride? You might think you know those answers, but unless you've tested the boundaries yourselves, you won't know. It's certainly not a figure that someone else has the answer for. Over the next few years we spurred each other on to do longer and harder rides, often for no other reason than 'why not.'

CHAPTER 3
Coast to Coast

Many long-distance cycling goals can be described as travelling from A to B. In the UK, there are two popular cycling goals. Land's End to John O'Groats – from south to north is LEJOG and north to south is the JOGLE – and there's the coast-to-coast (C2C) across the north of England. There's a variety of established routes for this (and you can, of course, create your own), but the most commonly ridden is probably the C2C. LEJOG is 874 miles long – it usually takes at least a week, but obviously could take longer. Devised by Sustrans, the C2C is around 100 miles long. It can be done in a day, but more commonly it's a two- to three-day ride.

It was October and Tom wanted to do a trip during his week-long, half-term school holiday. Through the year, since the Festive 500, we had ridden together generally once or twice a week, up to 25 miles or so. Tom had a cyclo-cross bike he rode on and off-road. He really wanted to do LEJOG, but I'd worked out it would need at least two weeks and we had only one week. I persuaded him otherwise, suggesting we did a C2C west to east, and then, if he wanted to, we could ride back again. We had a week, so there was no rush and there's a number of escape routes along the way if he changed his mind.

Our chosen route was 100 miles of the Hadrian's Cycleway, which loosely follows the line of the Roman Hadrian's Wall. We planned to camp or stay in bunkhouses and elected to start at Bowness-on-Solway near Carlisle early on the Saturday morning. Intent on an early start, we'd left home at 5.30am. Ann and Skye were driving us to the start of the ride and would pick us up from wherever we decided to finish. Nothing was cast in stone; we'd be as flexible as possible.

All was going well on the way to the start point until a tyre punctured on the turning off the M6 motorway. Not to worry. Confident I could change it in a flash, I was held up when the head of the bolt that secures the spare wheel sheared off. Still no worries as we have car recovery insurance. A quick phone call and we discover our cover has lapsed. A couple more calls, an hour's wait, and a recovery man arrived to release and fit the spare wheel. That would be the spare wheel with no air in it... Luckily the very nice recovery man had an air compressor. We were behind schedule, but only by a couple of hours. No worries. Well, there would have been no worries if the spare tyre had stayed inflated. As it was, we just managed to limp off the motorway before it went flat again.

Hopes were not high for a quick solution to the problem but after heading slowly towards Carlisle on three inflated tyres, I spied a tyre place where the original flat tyre and the spare tyre were replaced. After this, all that was left was a 40-minute drive to the start of our ride on the west coast where we rushed into our cycling kit. Ann took a quick photo, and we were away with just over five hours of daylight left to make an impression on our journey to the east coast.

The riding for the most part was on quiet roads and cycleways. Very pleasant. The weather was playing nicely, the temperature just above freezing and the sun was shining. The miles soon started to pass by. Arriving at Brampton after 20 miles the sun was noticeably low in the sky, but Tom and I decided that 20 miles didn't constitute a day's riding so staying there was discarded in favour of riding on to Haltwhistle. The route from Brampton was on quiet undulating roads – enjoyable riding and nothing too challenging, apart from a steep hill after the village of Greenhead. We'd hoped to reach Haltwhistle just before dusk and there was now some urgency as, although we had flashing lights, we hadn't brought lights to illuminate dark country roads. Back then Tom still had two speeds: 'moving' and 'not moving'. That might sound unfair, but the reality is that a seven-year-old doesn't have a fast touring speed that can be magically summoned – all you can hope for is that the bike is moving and not stopped. We made it to the outskirts of Haltwhistle just as the light was fading. I knew there was a campsite as I had stayed at it, albeit many years before. In the dark, however, finding it proved somewhat tricky. Eventually we saw a sign for a campsite, though not the one I'd been to. This was out of Haltwhistle, up a big hill. By then it was dark and there were no streetlights; our flashing lights did little to light our way. We were both more than happy when the turning into Herding Hill Farm campsite came into view. It was at that exact moment that it started to rain.

The owner gave us a friendly greeting and said they had tent pitches as well as some heated camping pods. The day had been long; we didn't take any persuading that a camping pod would be a far better idea than putting a tent up in the rain. Homemade pizza was on the menu, along with a Halloween party. Tom might have been up since 5am and cycled around 40 miles, but he wasn't going to miss a party.

The next morning we were greeted by more rain, exactly as forecast. When the campsite café opened we partook of a full English breakfast each. No children's portions for Tom. We'd planned a more leisurely day to the next destination, and stopped often for snacks and photographs. It was rather a bleak day, grey and windy, although we often saw bits of Hadrian's Wall, which added interest to the ride. We stopped for a café lunch at Corbridge with an enormous hot chocolate with marshmallows for Tom and arrived at our campsite that evening with lots of daylight to spare. None of the pubs in the immediate area did food on a Sunday evening, so we rode a couple of miles to Prudhoe to find a chip shop. Not the best chips in the world, but hot food on a night when the temperature was already below freezing was a necessity.

We woke early next morning to ice on the inside of the tent. There were only 23 flattish miles left to Tynemouth, our east coast destination. Not far enough for a full day's riding, so we decided to leave the tent at the campsite and ride to the sea and back in the afternoon. Tom was finding the miles easy.

The transition from countryside to the metropolis of Newcastle fascinated him. He made us cross the Gateshead Millennium Bridge, well, just because. Some lunch at the Cycle Hub café at Newcastle, then a few miles more, and we'd made it. Our first coast to coast was complete.

The ride back to camp was spent discussing our options for getting back to the west coast. By the time we'd finished the day we'd cycled 46 miles – Tom's longest ride so far.

While we had no particular time constraint on our return journey west, the weather forecast for two days ahead was heavy rain and strong westerly winds. When Tom was 7, his touring speed averaged out around 7.5 miles per hour. Our camp was 75 miles from our start/finish point on the west coast with 10 hours solid cycling – if we took 2 days to ride back we'd have to endure a day of heavy rain blowing into our faces. Still mulling it over, we set the alarm that night for a 6.15am start, although when the alarm rang, Tom decided to turn it off and go back to sleep without waking me. An hour later we awoke and had to rush to pack up; we were riding westwards by 7.30am, hoping to make the west coast by nightfall.

There was no time for café stops, instead we popped into a shop en route and bought a cake and a can of Coke to share. Tom was finding the riding easy and was super enthusiastic to be moving across the country again. The familiarity of the route, having already ridden it, helped to quantify our progress. The miles seemed to pass quickly. Unlike our first day, this was one when everything went according to plan. Just before dusk, we turned a corner and the Solway estuary came into view. That evening we stayed in a local bunkhouse and dined nearby at the Hope and Anchor. You might think Tom would've been exhausted, but no. After supper – with dessert, of course – he was still full of energy. Last orders were called at 11, with Tom still wanting another game of pool.

The following morning arrived with the promised heavy rain and wind; we were grateful not to be riding in it. Tom used the time while we waited for Ann to collect us to dream up some ideas for our next big ride – and I wouldn't have expected anything else.

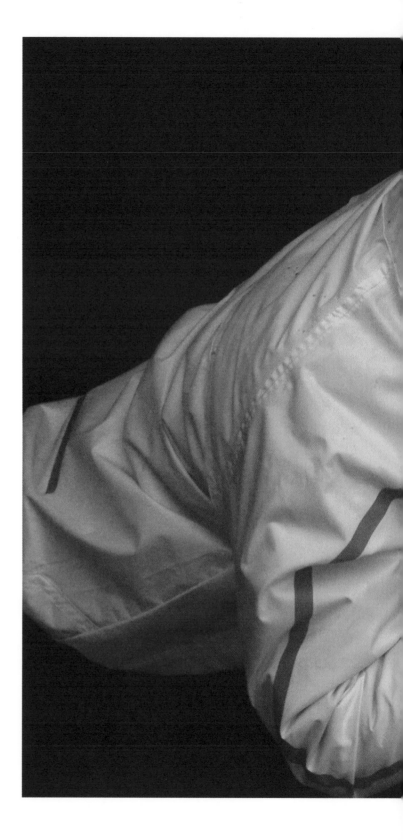

CHAPTER 4
Strathpuffer

They say that children can be adversely influenced by being exposed to certain parts of the internet at too young an age. So imagine my horror when I had a conversation with nine-year-old Tom after he had been browsing a cycling website and learnt that the winners of the Quad team at Strathpuffer one year were made up of kids aged thirteen and fourteen. Strathpuffer is a 24-hour mountain bike race that takes its name from the town of Strathpeffer, a few miles from Inverness in Scotland. The race is characterised by Scottish winter weather and a guaranteed 17 hours of darkness.

"Dad...?"

"Yes Tom."

"Can I ride at Strathpuffer?"

"I doubt it; I would've thought that you were too young. I'm fairly sure that the organisers won't let you."

Some years back I'd ridden Strathpuffer twice. Both times were tough. One race I finished, and one I didn't. To be honest I was in no rush to go back, but this wasn't my idea. Plus there was no chance they'd let him ride anyway. Right? Tom wouldn't take no for an answer though.

"Could you ask the organisers if a 13-year-old can ride at Strathpuffer, why can't I?"

A fair point. I sat down to write an email, though what should I say? I decide that a start would be to list Tom's achievements on a bike. Tom's first resumé. If he's to be in with a chance of a place, he'll need a CV that says 'this boy can'. I also added a bit about myself to persuade them that Tom would be accompanied by someone who knew what he was doing in a 24-hour race in winter.

We waited only a couple of days before we got a reply. To my surprise, it wasn't a flat 'no'. Instead a question: "Who else was going to be in Tom's team?" Our reply was that Tom didn't want to be in a team, he wanted to ride the 24 hours solo. Yes, this was in fact a 9-year-old who wanted to ride a 24-hour mountain bike race, solo, and in winter.

After another couple of days we got a reply saying that the other organisers would have to be consulted. A while later we got a further reply. Tom could ride Strathpuffer solo, though he would have to be accompanied every inch of the way by an adult, i.e. me. Tom was elated. I was happy for him, but apprehensive. Twenty-four hours on a bike in Scotland in winter is something I'd struggled with as an adult. I asked Tom if he really thought that he could do this. We'd need time off school, and would have to make plenty of other preparations.

It's funny how one's attitude changes to a race like this though. I wasn't going to be riding this for myself – I was going to be Tom's enabler, his right-hand man. I would have to step up. If Tom was going to ride one of the world's toughest bike races, I was going to make sure he could give it his absolute best shot. We travelled up to the race with some of Team JMC – Budge, Phil, Jacqui, Jason and his wife Debs. Jason was also riding the event and Debs had kindly offered to assist as our pit crew – throughout the 24 hours she would help us with food, drink, mechanical support and anything else we needed.

It was snowing as we drove through the Cairngorms and when we arrived at Strathpeffer there was snow. Tom was dismayed that the snow didn't make snowballs. The issue was that it was too cold, the temperature being -8°C.

We'd been contacted before the event by the makers of BBC's *The Adventure Show* who wanted to interview Tom about his Strathpuffer aspirations. We met up with them and Tom answered some questions for their feature. Dougie Vipond, one of the interviewers, had ridden the event as a soloist before. He'd really suffered and could only manage seven laps – I think they were somewhat taken aback by Tom's relaxed outlook on the event.

After helping get the Team JMC pit area ready, we adjourned to a nearby hotel for a warm night's sleep. The following morning we were up early. There was no time for pre-race nerves as we were rushing to make it to the start line on time. The start is a short run along a track, followed by finding your bike and then riding up a long fire road that climbs through the forest. Our planned tactics were to ride at a steady pace and – most importantly – not to crash. The course was coated in snow, with some icy patches, so the 'not crashing' bit proved quite tricky. Tom was fine on the descents and shallower climbs, though some of the steeper climbs were a challenge. But the trackside spectators were all cheering him on and the atmosphere was fantastic.

For the first few hours the sun was out, and it was an amazing experience to ride those trails in the snow. In winter this far north in Scotland, it isn't long into the race before the shadows lengthen. By 4.30pm the sun has gone. This is when the race really begins. The course seems to change as your field of view decreases. If things are not going well, then the darkness and cold will assist in magnifying your woes. If you've done a 24-hour race in summer you will have had around 4 hours of darkness during which to keep your demons at bay. At Strathpuffer there are over 17 hours of darkness to battle.

We'd had a conversation before putting in the entry as to what constitutes a solo 24-hour ride, and that is ride as far as you can in 24 hours. That means no sleep. In my experience, one thing that children like is sleep. The NHS website reckons a nine-year-old should be having ten hours sleep at night, which is a lot more than zero. We realised a concession might be needed, but Tom hoped not to stop for sleep.

It had just gone 1am when Tom started nodding off. We were maybe a third of the way up the first climb and he was fading. He'd been riding for 15 hours. I was expecting this may happen at some stage. We stopped and ate some Haribo, and I tried to infuse some enthusiasm in him. It was snowing, so I made sure we didn't hang about for long. A little further up and it became clear that Tom really did need some respite from the cold and the riding. I was about to suggest we turn around and go back down the hill when I remembered that there was a big marquee tent a little further up the hill, by the side of the course. The guys inside it were supporting other racers, but they'd had been cheering us on and had said to call in if we needed anything.

On arrival at their spread, we parked our bikes and went into their lovely warm tent which was outfitted with a big central wood burner and leather settees! I didn't have time to ask if we might stay awhile before Tom was fast asleep on one of the settees. I set my alarm for an hour, knowing that if we stopped much longer than that there was a possibility that Debs or the organisers might think we were in trouble.

Waking Tom once the hour was up was tough. He wasn't in snooze mode; he was in a deep sleep. Eventually he roused, had a cup of tea and a ham sandwich, and we were soon back out there. It would've been great if that hour's nap had done the trick, but when we arrived back at the timing tent it was obvious he needed more rest. We hadn't actually taken a tent, so ended up snoozing on chairs at the race HQ in front of a heater. You can ask what you will of your body but when you're a kid and it's time to sleep, that is the only option.

It was still dark when Tom woke for the second time and declared himself ready to get back out there. He'd hoped at the start to be able to ride 15 laps, which he'd been on target for quite a while. We rode a final lap as dawn broke to take Tom's total up to 10 laps, 64.9 miles and 8,000ft of climbing. Out of 92 solo riders Tom came 61st.

Tom was very pleased to be awarded the Doug Stewart memorial award for youth performance which is given to the best Under-19 rider. He got a standing ovation as he received his trophy. There may have been a tear in my eye.

After packing our stuff into the van, we went for a burger and had a few hours' sleep in a hotel before heading to the local restaurant. Tom ate his supper then fell asleep in the restaurant.

Tom dug deep that day in tough conditions. Even so, it wasn't long before Tom was talking about heading back to the 'Puffer to give it another go and improve on his ride. We have since returned six times.

THE HIGHLAND TRAIL

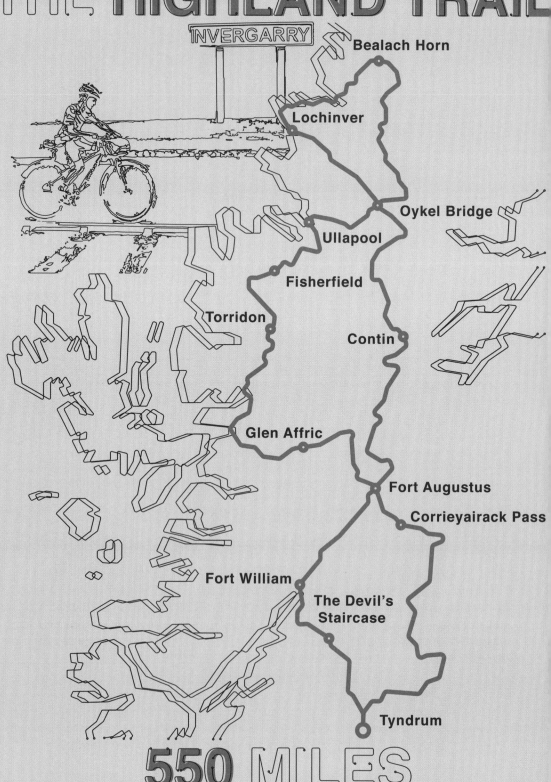

INVERGARRY

Bealach Horn

Lochinver

Oykel Bridge

Ullapool

Fisherfield

Torridon

Contin

Glen Affric

Fort Augustus

Corrieyairack Pass

Fort William

The Devil's Staircase

Tyndrum

550 MILES

CHAPTER 5
Highland Trail

Buoyed up by being accepted for a place on the Strathpuffer, Tom looked around for other things we could do. Tom's age means nothing to him and is most certainly not going to be an obstacle to what he might achieve on a bike if he so wishes.

The previous year I'd taken part in the Highland Trail 550. The '550' are the miles, the 'Highland' bit refers to the Highlands of Scotland. The challenge itself a self-timed Individual Time Trial (ITT) with no prizes and no support. The route is for mountain bikes. Reaching some fairly remote places, it is a Grand Tour of the Highlands, designed by a rider called Alan Goldsmith, an understated and funny character who is one of the most experienced bikepackers in the UK.

Bikepacking events are always low-key. Some of the very fastest riders do them but, given the lack of prizes, not for the money. The events are generally tough challenges through remote lands and the progress of riders who choose to carry a satellite tracker can be watched by anyone online throughout their challenge. 'Dotwatching' is the term for this, and it has become a popular pastime during some of the larger bikepacking events.

Starting in Tyndrum on the West Highland Way, the Highland Trail does a big anticlockwise loop. The loop meets Fort Augustus and then Oykel Bridge and goes through both twice. Furthest north is Bealach Horn in Sutherland, where on a clear day you can see the sea off the northernmost points of Scotland. Heading back south, although the mileage halfway point comes soon, the effort needed to return to Tyndrum is less than half done. I'd completed this route in just under the competitive time limit of eight days and I put it up there with the toughest things I've achieved. With some mechanical issues early on, I had to nurse my bike to get to the end. I guess it was as mentally stressful as it was physical, and at one stage I'd considered pulling out. What kept me going though, was asking myself what Tom would do – would he pack up and go home? Only a third of the starters finished that year, and I was proudly one of them.

Tom asked to me get in touch with Alan Goldsmith. Along with designing the route Alan organises a group depart that takes place the weekend before the Spring Bank Holiday at the end of May. In bikepacking parlance, 'group depart' is a time and a place for a number of people to embark on a challenge such as the Highland Trail, as opposed to an individual attempt that can be embarked upon at any time. Tom wanted to know if he could join in and ride by my side. I'd have to get in touch with Alan then. An email was sent. Back then I didn't know Alan well, and he'd never heard of Tom. Unsurprisingly, he said he thought it was a less than good idea for someone of Tom's age to consider riding such a challenging route. I guess if it wasn't for the fact that I'd completed the route, he'd have thought my request really crazy. Anyway, from then on he kept an eye on what riding Tom was doing.

When you're at school, rides like the Highland Trail have to fit into school holidays. As an adult if you don't have a place on a group start it's polite to avoid it and do your own ride at a different time, but we didn't have that luxury. Given that the group depart of the Highland Trails always begins on the Saturday before the second bank holiday Monday in May (when in England the week-long half-term school holiday also always falls), the best we could manage was starting a day before everyone else.

We'd hoped to be up and away earlier on the first day, but faffed about getting ready and it had just gone 7am when we left Tyndrum. Our friends Marion and Kevin had come to see us off, which was lovely – Kevin is a fellow cyclist and Marion is famed for being a dotwatcher – but we were soon alone as we rode towards Rannoch Moor. The weather was substandard – windy, cold, raining on and off. But we were dressed for the weather and got on with it. The first big climb of the day was over the Devil's Staircase towards Kinlochleven. With our bikes fully laden, we were soon off and pushing. From the road to the col the trail climbs 250m in approximately 1,500m. The surface is rocky and sometimes loose and Tom found it tough. This must have been obvious to walkers on the path as on more than one occasion a walker offered to push his bike for him. Which, of course, he politely declined.

Tom revelled in the technical descent down to Kinlochleven, and we were soon ensconced in the café there. Tea and toasted cheese and ham sandwiches were quickly consumed, and we were soon heading uphill again. The climb isn't a long one and we enjoyed riding along Loch Eilde Mor. The rain had ceased, but conditions were definitely still damp with surface water everywhere. At the end of this track I knew our feet were going to get a bit wetter for here at Luibeilt was a river – the Abhainn Rath. We needed to be on the other side, and yes, you've guessed it, there is no bridge. The previous year, the river was little more than ankle deep when I'd crossed. This year, though, shall we say it looked a little livelier. Personally I have a very healthy dislike for fast-moving water. In fact, regarding my wishes about involvement in water, I'm happy to draw the line at heated swimming pools... other than a bath, of course. Needs must though on this route, and this is but a trickle as far as rivers on the Highland Trail are concerned.

Tom had absolutely no experience of crossing rivers, either with or without a loaded bike, and did I mention he couldn't swim? I don't recall Tom being especially concerned about this, but decided to help him anyway. I scoped what looked like the best line across and, leaving my bike behind, lowered his bike down into the water. Tom steered his bike diagonally downstream of himself, and we made steady progress. Nearing the far side a stronger current grabbed his bike, which in turn threatened to drag him over with it. I quickly grabbed him and then his saddle. It was a touch more exciting than I liked – I was relieved when we made it to the other side and I'd got him and his bike out of the water.

Once I'd undramatically retrieved my own bike we embarked on an hour and a half of dragging and shoving our bikes along the other side of the river to cover three miles. We followed the purple line on the GPS hoping for a trail, but never really finding one. We recrossed the bridge at Loch Treighead and headed for Loch Ossian in the late afternoon sunshine. I vaguely recall someone saying you could get a drink at the Ossian Youth Hostel, so we diverted slightly there. As it turned out they didn't really do drinks, but the warden kindly made us a cup of tea anyway.

To get to the YHA we'd been riding for over 12 hours, but Tom was feeling good. In fact he was probably already fed up with me pestering him to see if he was tired, thirsty, hungry... We decided to keep riding until it got dark, and then find somewhere to put the tent up. The year before it hadn't taken me long to ride the section from Ossian to the Melgarve bothy where I'd spent the night, so we discussed making the bothy our goal. I told Tom of the fire and the comfy settee I'd slept on there. Darkness came, and Tom decided that his first night in a bothy was something worth riding on for. We fired up our lights and rode on.

Not far from the bothy, I pulled up to get out some snacks to tide us over and told Tom to 'just follow the road'. Snacks retrieved, I jumped on the pedals to catch Tom up. Weirdly I couldn't see him, but spotted a moving light in the distance. He'd seen some house lights, and turned off towards them; he must have smashed it to get that far so fast. I sprinted to catch him up – he was adamant it was the bothy and said he'd 'raced' to get there as quickly as possible.

We were still seven miles away from the bothy though. Tom had spent his calories, and that last stretch took about an hour. On arrival I helped him get out his PJs and quickly tucked him up in his sleeping bag, simultaneously feeding him fig roll biscuits. We chatted, but he was asleep as soon as his head touched the settee he'd been looking forward to. I had the foresight to remove the remains of the unchewed fig roll from his mouth before I bedded down next to him. He'd ridden 85 miles that day, exactly the same as I and several others had achieved the year before, though in worse conditions. Prior to beginning the Highland Trail, he thought that if he got that far the first day we could finish in under eight days.

Maybe we'd gone too hard, too early? Tom had certainly dug deep. I wondered if this was going to be sustainable for another week.

The next morning we were greeted by blue skies. A great start to the day. We had a bit of a lie-in as I was mindful that Tom had done a tough day's riding. For today we'd just see where we'd get to with no particular target except, of course, the pizza shop in Fort Augustus. First, though, we'd have to climb over the 770m Corrieyairack Pass. It's mostly rideable until some zigzags just before the top. At the top of these we had to traverse a snowfield where Tom made snowballs to throw at me. On the way down we sought out another bothy for no reason other than future reference.

Our leisurely morning saw us in the pizza shop early doors. We both ordered big pizzas – the waiter not at all convinced that Tom would finish his. Tom, of course, ate every crumb, and then some of mine as he was still hungry. Grown-up bike riding requires grown-up food portions. We bought supplies from the shop and then headed north again at whatever pace Tom wanted to go. It was clear that today was going to be easier, and that was fine with me. We had a whole week to enjoy Scotland's riding.

That night's bothy had everything going for it, with a fireplace and wood and some big polystyrene sheets to sleep on. We lit a fire and spent a couple of hours enjoying being dry and warm. I warned Tom as we settled down to sleep that we might be woken in the middle of the night by riders coming through at the front end of the group start, and so it was. Tom slept through all the arrivals and departures until Alan Goldsmith showed up. Alan had called in simply to say hi to Tom, shake his hand, and congratulate him on his progress. I could tell Alan was genuinely impressed that a child had ridden so far.

Next day there was wind and the occasional squally shower to accompany us. We spent plenty of time chatting with riders who caught us up as we rode towards Contin, which is a major resupply point on the route. Once there, we found a group of riders including cycling writer Dave Barter. We shared our stories so far, and it was good to also catch up later on at Inchbae Lodge with Alan Parkinson whom I'd met on my first Highland Trail. We did a good deal of sitting around and chatting to others that day – for us, these events are as much about the people you meet as they are about the riding.

After Contin we briefly covered some familiar tracks we'd last ridden in the snow at Strathpuffer. By mid-afternoon I knew any chance we possibly had of completing the route inside eight days had expired. There was, however, an easy plan B. Two years before there had been no northern '550' loop, just a shorter 440 route, so instead of heading north at Oykel Bridge, we could miss out 110 miles and simply resume the shared route towards Ullapool.

We camped that night in the shadow of some ruins at Lubachlaggan. It was windy and wet, but we stayed dry. The next day, it seemed the weather was punishing us for taking an easier route towards Ullapool, and it rained more and the wind blew even harder. We were grateful for bacon sandwiches at the Oykel Bridge Hotel. We saw Tom Rowntree there – that year's eventual winner. He spoke of hardly being able to stand up on the northern loop, so I was grateful we'd decided to give it a miss.

The rain slackened off in the afternoon, but the wind continued to fight with us. We went for some luxury that evening and stayed at the campsite with supper at a nearby Indian restaurant. We ate our fill. It was a good evening, but sitting opposite Tom, though I could see the joy in his eyes, his face looked weathered way beyond his years.

Scotland had left its mark on him for all to see, but the route's party piece was definitely still to come – the dangerous river crossing in Fisherfield.

Up early the next day, we headed into town to grab some supplies from the shop. There was a fully packed bike outside and inside we found someone we know – Javi – wearing his usual beaming smile. We exchanged a few words, but we were all in a hurry. The weather was again wind and rain showers. Nothing much if you were just out doing some shopping, but more than an inconvenience where we were heading next.

From Ullapool there's a proper road with traffic, which is a bit rubbish, though as we headed towards the turn-off to the start of the next section, the traffic was incidental to my thoughts. More important was remembering the route and breaking it down for Tom so he could visualise what were basically going to be some tough times ahead.

First up: the 'coffin road'. Now a historian will say that this path was named thus as it was a route for carting dead people from A to B. Why you would want to carry a dead person over a big hill is a mystery to me, having pushed a loaded bike up there. Tom struggled from the start. Hell, I struggled too. Surface water made grip marginal. I ended up pushing my bike up a section, then going back down to help Tom push his bike. The technique was push the bike forward, apply brakes, release brakes, then push up again, hoping that you don't lose your footing and end up with your bike on top of you. We made it to the top, but it was ridiculously slow progress.

Part of my unfolding story of the route for Tom was about the sweet descent down towards Dundonell. How wrong I was. We pushed nearly as much heading downhill as we had when pushing up. Everything was waterlogged; progress was painfully slow.

Dropping into the valley we met Rickie and Stefan who were on the 550 trail. Rickie shared out sweets and for a short while we laughed and smiled. But there were thoughts of what was over the next hill where the crux of the route through the Fisherfield Forest is a wide river crossing. In good weather you can pedal across with dry feet, but it can become truly impassable when it's wet. After that is a remote section that would be a long push in wet weather. The fatigue on Rickie and Stefan's faces reminded me how much effort we'd all put into getting to this point, and how little room for error there is in these remote places. It was decision time for Tom and me so we wished them good luck and, while they headed on, we took to the road heading south. Over the next two and a half days we did a mix of road and Highland Trail back to Tyndrum to complete our total of 405 wet and windy miles.

We hadn't finished what we'd set out to do, but Tom now had some experience of the Highland Trail. Throughout the ride we had between us made sensible decisions, taking into account Tom's energy levels, the terrain, and the weather. I knew at some stage he'd want to go back and complete what he had started. I was impressed by his resolve. Riding a multi-day trip such as the Highland Trail is tough for anyone. It's especially harder for someone like Tom, considering how his weight compares to that of his bike. But that big first day showed us that with a bit more stamina and strength, a child could finish the Highland Trail in under eight days. Tom was keen to prove that to Alan Goldsmith.

CHAPTER 6
An Imperial Century

Tom had wanted to do a ride of 100 miles for a while. Their first imperial century is a landmark for any rider. I can still remember when I did mine; I was much older than Tom! Having completed rides of 70 and 80 miles a few times already without any drama, he felt this was a milestone that should be ticked off. But instead of this decision being made in the summer when we'd have long days and at least the chance of warm weather, of course, we chose November to do his first 100.

Familiar miles are great for big distances like this. No surprises needed. We knew just the route – it would be on the Hadrian's Wall Cycleway, which we'd already ridden over a few days. Part of this is exactly 100 miles coast to coast, so that would do nicely. Our plan was to ride to Tynemouth on the Saturday, then ride back on the Sunday. We were going to travel light, so I booked a hotel on the east coast – no camping equipment needed on this trip.

Looking at the weather forecast the night before the ride, I guess I was optimistic – it didn't look great. Snow showers were forecast, but the alarm was set for 2.45am anyway. We packed clothes fit for the worst weather and retired to bed. Tom and I were quickly up, dressed and fed with the bikes in the car ready to drive north and, as we hit the road, on came the snow and sleet. Tom checked the weather and traffic reports on my phone as I drove – the roads were open as far as we could tell. Onwards.

There were a couple of brief moments on the M6 motorway which suggested that 'onwards' wasn't such a good idea. With one lane of the motorway closed, the gritters and snowploughs were at work. Luckily, the snow showers quickly abated and by Carlisle the road was clear. I was, for a while at least, pleased that we'd taken a chance with the weather.

We arrived at Bowness on Solway and in a few minutes the bikes were ready to ride, and so were we. It was still dark and the temperature was close to freezing, but we had the clothes for the job. We'd done this bit before and it was great to be riding on a familiar route. Firing up our lights, we rode eastwards.

Three years before when we first rode this route Tom had been much slower, so it was great to see how much stronger he had become on his bike. It meant we had breakfast number two in Carlisle much earlier than I'd thought we would, savouring pork pies in the car park. We worked out that even with a couple of breaks we should be at our hotel well before dark. There was no rush.

As you leave Carlisle on the Hadrian's Cycleway the route soon leaves busy roads, and starts to climb slowly. I started to notice isolated patches of ice on the ungritted road and mentioned it to Tom, though he'd already spotted the white bits. There were even a few tiny bits of snow on the verges. It looked pretty, and at that stage was no more than the countryside wearing its glistening early morning make-up. It wasn't more than a couple of miles further when it became clear that this pretty white stuff was going to be a bit of a nuisance. We were now having to look for the lines of most friction on the deserted roads, instead of just avoiding the odd patch of ice.

As they say, things quickly escalated. We turned onto a section of road where the surface was all ice. Snow that had fallen on the tarmac had briefly melted and frozen again. I tried riding on the grass verge with some success while Tom did his best to stay upright on the road, which led to three falls in quick succession. We pushed our bikes, hoping we'd soon get to a road that had been treated with grit. Back on a section that was rideable slowly with caution, things were looking up again. The sun was out and the sky was blue, but as we continued to climb, conditions got worse for cycling and better for ice skating or cross-country skiing. The ice was now accompanied by a good half inch of snow.

Stopping for some food at a milepost 25 miles from where we had started, we still had another 75 miles to go. Via some friends on Twitter, I learned that continuing would be futile as there were reports of ice and snow the whole way along our route. We hadn't expected this. We'd thought that this ride was going to be straightforward and all we'd need to do was pedal. Disappointingly, Tom's imperial century wasn't going to happen. Taking a break to eat, we mulled over our options. With 25 miles done, we'd have to ride the same at least to get back to the car. Fifty miles – only half of what we'd hoped to achieve for the day. We took a more direct route back to Carlisle on main roads to avoid the ice we'd earlier encountered and on the other side of Carlisle the roads were free of ice – I guess proximity to the sea and the lack of altitude had kept the temperature up.

I suggested to Tom that if he wanted to complete the 100 miles there could be a way and his spirits immediately lifted. My idea was to retrace our route to the car, stash our overnight gear and then head south, keeping close to the sea and hopefully avoiding any more of the white stuff. Tom was keen, so we navigated south using the compass on our GPS. We were treated to quiet roads and afternoon sunshine, but as we neared our turnaround point with 75 miles done, Tom started asking the classic 'are we there yet'. It was a longer, harder day than we'd planned for.

The odometer read 76 miles as we rolled into the small village of Allonby, which is about 10 miles north of the Lake District. Turning round to head back to the car, we spied a chip shop and it was open. There was only one course of action. We ordered a tray of chips and a can of Coke each. The guy running the shop also gave Tom a candy cane off the Christmas tree. We enjoyed the food, the hospitality, and the warmth inside the shop.

Fuelled with food and knowing there's only a couple of hours on now-familiar roads, we headed back north. It was a bit of a rollercoaster of a day and we reflected on the weather conditions we'd encountered. The last hour of the ride was in darkness, during which we debated where we'd eat before we drove back down south. Getting back to the car at 5pm, we'd ridden 102 miles. I put the bikes in the back of the car and Tom googled for the nearest Pizza Hut. Century ride done, now it's all about the pizza!

Looking back, it would have been easy to have stayed home in the Peak District on that November morning because the weather was certainly not on our side. And when we encountered the snow and ice and things definitely weren't going according to plan, we could have just turned round and headed home. But Tom and I worked out a way of achieving our goal of riding 100 miles in spite of the obstacles and we are both proud of that.

CHAPTER 7
Devils and Angels

You'll remember the tale of Tom's first Festive 500 in chapter two. Ride five hundred kilometres in eight days over the Christmas period age seven? Yep, done that. The following year we'd done the 500k again, though with an added concurrent Strava challenge of running 33 miles as if the 500 wasn't test enough. The running challenge started two days before the Festive 500 so we'd already run 13 miles by the time the Festive 500 commenced. The rest of the running we fitted in either before or after our riding. We did all the runs from our front door, taking the opportunity to run around and about Kinder Scout – the highest hill in the Peak District – visiting parts of its expansive plateau that aren't accessible by bike.

In 2014 we had another go at the Festive 500, but both of us started off suffering some kind of lurgy, sacking it after two days and 125km as we felt so ill. No doubt we could have pushed on to finish the challenge, but neither of us were enjoying it. Enough said.

We started to plan our fourth Festive 500, even though we faced time constraints. Relatives from Australia would be in London from December 27th and we'd be busy on Christmas Day. That gave us three full days as a starting point – the 24th, 26th and 27th. It had only been a month since Tom's first imperial century so I planned a fairly flat, if long, ride for the first day. Life doesn't always have to be hard.

We rode out to the east coast with a following westerly wind, but it was nearly all over for me in Sheffield. Nearing the city I'd warned Tom about tram tracks and what happens when your front wheel gets caught in them. Minutes later I slipped into the rails and was pitched to the ground. The impact was taken by my shoulder and hip. A sigh of relief as nothing broken, but I was very sore.

We stopped for breakfast at 9am, having already ridden 75km. As we left the café it began to rain and then it absolutely hammered down. The roads turned into rivers of surface water in seconds. For some reason, car drivers saw no need to slow down, so we got out of the way and onto the pavement until the rain calmed down a bit and the roads cleared of water.

The rain ran away from us after a couple of hours, and the last few miles towards the east coast were quite pleasant. The ride was, unusually, very flat as I'd taken care to make it 'easy'. Tom commented on how boring the riding was without hills...

As we neared our destination of Hornsea, the sun came out. A quick photo on the seafront and then we went in search of Ann and Skye who'd driven over to pick us up.

At 176km, we'd done well over a third of our target. Christmas day at Granny's was great, and for the first time in a few years no bikes were ridden.

We had to be in London for the 28th and we live in the Peak District, which Google Maps tells me is 199 miles away. I guess you can work out where we headed next. Rapha organises a Manchester to London ride each year in aid of an autism charity, and it was around their route that we chose to ride south. The first day was going to be the longer of the two – at nearly 200km it was by far the furthest Tom had ridden. Having said that, we always find that going a little bit further than the last big ride is always achievable. At least there'd be no snow and ice.

We set off early in the dark and the rain. Our lights kept us illuminated and we had the right clothes to keep us warm and dry. In the dark, the puddles looked like river fords. Suffice to say there was plenty of water around. At Carsington Water we stopped at the café for a second breakfast – full cooked English, of course. The rain eventually stopped and, though there was a headwind, we enjoyed the riding. Mostly quiet lanes took us towards Northampton where we'd booked a roadside hotel for the night. As soon as we arrived we arranged a pizza delivery for supper, ordering more than enough 'just in case' and some of that became next morning's first breakfast. We were both tired after a long day, but in excellent spirits.

Still a bit tired when the alarm went off at 6am, we had a bit of a lie-in and left just after 9am. We could afford to be a bit lazy as we'd only 130km left to ride that day. The destination was our accommodation in London and we weren't expected until early evening. The weather was again damp, though I can't say it bothered us. We chatted about this and that as we rode through the middle of the UK on surprisingly quiet roads. After the last of two café stops, darkness wasn't far away and we fired up our lights – Tom lit up like a Christmas tree. Hertfordshire lanes took us towards the outskirts of London. At around 5pm, our Festive 500 was all but done with maybe 15km left to ride.

And then we'd just dropped down a small roller of a hill and were climbing up the other side with me in front of Tom when I heard a car approaching fast. The road was wide though and it wouldn't be the first time a car had driven faster than it should as it passed us. A second or so later, and I heard a quiet thud – the car flashed past, closely followed by another. They were driving around 50 to 60 miles an hour and appeared to be racing. Almost simultaneously as they passed, I heard Tom scream. Turning round, I could see his front bike light was static and pointing down to the ground.

He's not moving. Is this how it ends? Riding a bike, doing what he loves? I'm probably only 20 metres in front but it takes an eternity to get to him. He's crying. Heart stops. I don't swear, but I'm thinking it. He isn't moving, but he is alive.

He's obviously been hit by one of the cars. His rear bike wheel was folded in half and his helmet smashed. He's been launched forwards onto the grass verge, still clipped into the pedals.

I find some calm and quickly give him a once-over. I can't find any blood and it appears that although his helmet and bike are broken, none of his bones are. Relief.

I phone for an ambulance, but weirdly a police car arrives while I'm still on the phone. They help me get Tom comfy while we wait for the paramedics. These officers already know what happened as they'd had a call from a motorist who'd been driving behind a car that was swerving along the road. Apparently they'd managed to get in front of the erratic driver, taken his keys away and held them until another police unit had arrived.

The emotion of the situation comes to me when I call my wife to say: "There's been an incident; Tom's been hit by a car, but he appears to be OK..."

We wait a considerable while for the ambulance, which isn't a complaint, just an observation. Tom's self-diagnosis is the only really sore bit is his ankle. He can move it. "No problem, it's just sore." I'm mindful that he could go into shock, so I chat about all sorts of randomness to try to distract him from what has just happened. As the conversation progresses Tom says he's annoyed that we were within 15km of completing another Festive 500, and instead he had a bike that wasn't going to be ridden anywhere in its current state.

The paramedics arrive and give Tom the all-clear with an advisory that if his ankle doesn't settle that he has it X-rayed. While we wait for Ann to collect us, Tom asks if we know anyone in London who has a small bike. I can see where he's heading with this. I put out a request on Twitter for friends to ask their friends if anyone would be kind enough to loan us a bike and a helmet for a couple of hours the following day somewhere in London. As the saying goes 'Twitter, do your thing'. It did.

Helen (a friend of our friend Nick) came to the rescue and we arranged to go to her apartment in central London at 10am. Our plan was to borrow the bike, ride 15km round London then give Helen her bike back. Easy. The logistics required a little thought – I had a bike and Tom didn't, so we got a cab into town. Lovely Helen kindly offered to take us out for a spin and show us the town along with her husband Mark. This was excellent, as we got to see many of London's sights and in fact, ended up riding a good deal further than 15km that day.

Over the years there have been a number of 'that was close' incidents, and though we've always tried to reduce the chances of being mowed down by a car, the reality is that Tom through no fault of his own was very unlucky that day. I have to say that following this incident our desire to ride on roads in the UK definitely lessened. Thankfully there's plenty of off-road riding in the UK and some excellent road riding in mainland Europe.

The driver of the car was charged with driving with excess alcohol, and leaving the scene of an accident. His sentence was in line with what others get – a mere slap on the wrist. There are some selfish people out there and some generous people. Try to avoid the former.

So Tom did finish his third Festive 500. His words just after the crash? "It's great to be alive."

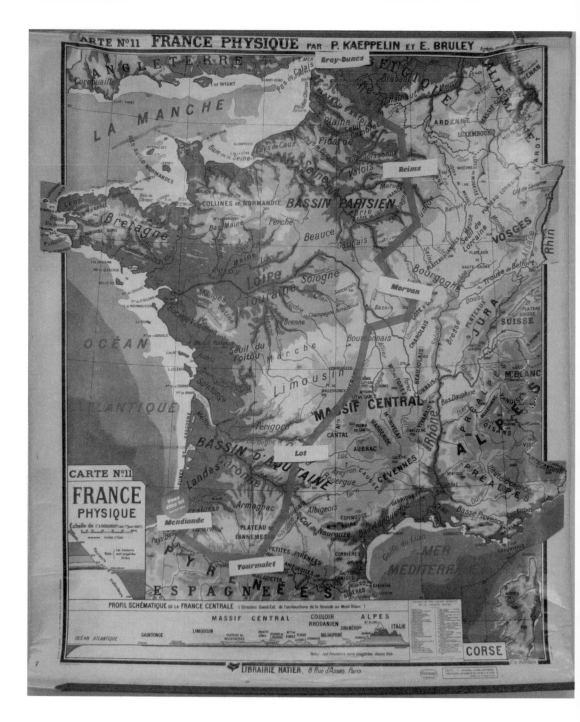

CHAPTER 8
Steak Bleu

A question Tom and I are often asked is 'What's next'. While 'next' is most likely a quick hour after school, for the last few years there has been a big goal. One of the ultimate bike trips: the 2,750-mile Tour Divide, a route which starts in Banff in Canada and ends on the Mexican border following the Continental Divide as it heads south.

I'd met Dave Hanney, the CEO of Alpkit, at a party and off the back of our conversation they built us a tandem on which we could ride the Tour Divide. It seemed sensible that Tom (aged 11) and I went and did something long, but a little closer to home as training. While in theory I thought we'd be able to ride the Tour Divide back then, I was intimidated by the thought of going out there and failing. We'd always made small steps to longer and harder trips. So in the summer of 2016 Tom and I were looking for something big, but a bit closer to home.

We'd noticed a new route that year – the French Divide. This crosses France from the NE to the SW corner, and is approximately 2,000km long. The organisers of the route kindly let us have their GPX track so we could see where it went. We began to devise a plan of sorts.

At the beginning of Tom's school holidays we would be doing a talk in Bromsgrove about our cycling trips, so we decided our ride could start there. Then we'd have a two-day ride to the Dover to Dunkerque ferry and a short ride along the coast to the start in Bray-Dunes near the Belgian border. We were to ride across France, but how were we going to get back from the southwest of France? Ferry, plane, or the easiest to organise, ride? Yep, so we'd planned to ride back too.

Those 2,000 miles would be a good test of us, our tandem and our equipment. If we managed to ride it without mishap we knew we'd have a chance of completing the Tour Divide.

Tom and I had the tandem for nearly a year and though we'd ridden it a fair bit, had never actually ridden it very far in a single ride. We made up for that on the first day by riding 221km to stay with Andy, a friend and fellow cyclist in London. By the time we neared Dover on the second day, for the first time ever I got blister on my butt. Unlike on a solo bike, when you ride a tandem on the road, you sit for the most part in one position on the saddle – maybe that had been the cause. It wasn't exactly painful, whatever the reason, but it was certainly uncomfortable.

As well as that problem, we encountered some issues with the tandem. It had been increasingly difficult to pedal. After some investigation we found out that one of the bottom bracket bearings (which support the pedal's axle) had collapsed. A replacement was needed. We hadn't even made it as far as France and already things were going wrong. We spent time at a chain store in Dover trying to source the required part, but eventually conceded we'd do better finding one on the other side of the English Channel.

Later that afternoon in Dunkerque we searched for an open bike shop, but with little success. In the evening at the Bray-Dunes campsite where other French Divide riders would congregate over the next couple of days, we met one of the British riders, Steve Heading. He suggested trying one of the bike shops in Belgium and next morning drove us over the border. Success. We bought two bottom brackets, fitted one, thanks again to Steve's help, and stashed the other as a spare.

Just after lunch, we headed south. The route on the first couple of days followed the Belgium-France border, meandering between both countries. We passed several reminders of the First and Second World Wars. The sun shining through the trees as we rode the tandem up the Kemmelberg's cobbles towards The Angel monument was magical.

We weren't official French Divide racers. Our original plan was to set off a full day ahead of the other riders. Instead, by the end of our first day we were maybe only seven hours ahead of the racers. The following day, although we were away early, we were soon overtaken by Ben Steurbaut, the fastest rider. The rest of that day and the following day we were passed by everyone else. It was lovely meeting and chatting to the people from many different countries who'd come to take on this ride, many of whom we now call friends.

We met the event organisers at the first checkpoint at Reims, but were too late to make the second checkpoint cut-off. Our progress on the tandem was much slower than we'd thought it would be. This was a lesson that made me realise that our Tour Divide aspirations might need to be put on hold. For this trip though, it didn't really matter. We rode shorter days than the racers, but were still averaging around 130km a day.

The weather as we headed south became warmer each day. By the time we reached the Morvan National Park it was really hot, not something we were used to. In retrospect we'd have benefited from having a couple of extra bottles on the bike; we seemed to be always on the search for water. I was having mild knee issues coupled with an ever-present pain from that blister, though an excellent blister plaster did help a bit – thanks Tom for assisting with that!

Progress on the steep sandy hills in the Morvan was glacial. We chatted as we rode, but all our energies on that hot afternoon were mostly devoted to forward motion. I asked Tom if he was still enjoying himself, but 'no, not really'. I knew the riding from there would only get tougher, as we'd not yet visited the biggest hills of the route. We discussed our options. Number one was continue the route, two was head home and admit defeat, and three was leave the route and take an easier way south to the French-Spanish border. The first and second choices were swiftly discarded.

It was at that moment that we ceased following the French Divide route. A weight of sorts was lifted from our shoulders. Not that we covered any fewer miles over the following days, it was just that we took a route with less physical resistance. Our daily routine continued. Ride, eat, sleep, repeat. A simple way of life.

This was the first time Tom and I had been away for such a long time with just the two of us. Some days we'd chat incessantly, and other days we'd speak little. We got on well, bearing in mind we were tied together during the day by the tandem and by night in a shared tent. I tried to ensure that Tom had his say in decisions as to how far we rode and where we stayed each night.

Food became our passion. We'd taken no cooking equipment and relied on finding a hot meal at some stage of the day. Breakfast was usually as many pastries and cakes we could eat from a boulangerie. Lunch was baguette-based with whatever filling grabbed us. Tom happily tries new foods. Steak tartare was favourite if eating out, and tinned mackerel fillets in a mustard sauce with a baguette at the roadside.

I've visited France a fair few times, but this route didn't touch the usual tourist places that I'd been before. Canal towpaths, farm tracks, quiet roads, and just a general feeling that France is a big country where not so many people live once you're out of the towns and cities. We both enjoyed this France.

One afternoon we had a lengthy conversation about Tom living in France when he was older. He was clearly smitten with the place. We chatted about what he might do one day for a career to allow him to live there. People often ask him if one day he'd like to be a professional bike rider. The pros and cons of being a professional rider were talked about. Cycling for us was always about having fun. Would being a pro cyclist be fun? Instead, what about a job that paid well and would allow him to buy a bike to ride where and when he wanted. What jobs could he do that would allow him to do that? There were lots of suggestions, but Tom liked the idea of international lawyer. I still don't know what I want to do when I'm grown up, and here is Tom at the age of 11 looking at suggestions for a career. It's wonderful on these long trips that we can have lengthy conversations that we'd not normally have a chance to have.

A couple of days after leaving the French Divide route we'd sort of forgotten about it, concentrating instead of making our own route southwest. On the 19th of August I got a message from Céline (one of the French Divide organisers) to say we were still invited to the finisher's party in Mendionde on the following day. As we were only about 100km away, that became the plan for the next day. We arrived the following afternoon to be greeted by the organisers and those riders who had already finished. A beer for me and a Coke for Tom were placed in our hands. We spent the afternoon and evening swapping stories with the other riders. I watched Tom chatting confidently with these adults – they treated him not as a child, but as a young man who'd battled his way to get to this place just as they had.

The following morning it rained for the first time. It was a pleasurable change from the overbearing heat of the last few days, but it didn't last. By the time we'd arrived on the Atlantic coast the sun was baking our backs once again.

We took the tandem onto the beach and dipped our toes briefly in the sea before heading north. We still had 1,000km to go to take us back to the ferry. The character of the riding was very different. We left behind quiet roads and sleepy villages for a traffic-free route called La Vélodyssée that hugged the coast. It was traffic-free, but being close to sandy beaches was busy with sun worshipping beachgoers.

We were heading home and though we weren't in a rush to be finished, it was good to know that the hard miles were behind us. With just over 400km left, Ann suggested that she could come and collect us from Portsmouth but only if we could be there in three days. Challenge accepted, we put in some longer days. On the final day Tom was tiring, but quickly perked up when I suggested that if we made St Malo by nightfall we could stay in a hotel. The feeling of the Egyptian cotton sheets in that hotel that night after being in sleeping bags for over a month was wonderful. Tom still talks about the rare steak we ate that evening. Steak bleu has become a firm favourite for him.

While we hadn't completed the entire French Divide route, we had ridden 3,226km, and successfully dealt with the tandem's mechanical woes. We had also proven to ourselves that our bodies could deal with riding day after day without resting. The best thing about the whole trip was that we had a really good time in each other's company. But we'd not been as quick on the tandem as I thought we would be, especially on the hilly bits. This concerned me as the Tour Divide has lots of hilly bits...

On our return from France, Tom and I were asked by the Alpkit guys if we could do a presentation at their Big Shakeout festival in September outlining what we'd been up to over the summer. We had only done a couple of talks before, and this would be to the largest number of people by far. I asked Tom if he fancied it, to which he replied 'yes'. I generally avoid having to stand up in front of a crowd of people. When I was Tom's age, I found the prospect terrifying. But, if Tom was up for it, I'd have to quell my nerves and give it a shot. As preparation we gathered up some pictures of our trip. We then spent a couple of evenings reminding ourselves where and what each picture signified. Tom wanted me to be the one who introduced us, but otherwise Tom was happy to chip in with his own view on events.

We were definitely nervous at the beginning, but both relaxed as the talk progressed. One part of our tale that the crowd loved was an account of when we arrived at a large campsite not far from Biarritz. I say 'large', but perhaps a better description would be 'massive'. This place had 1,400 pitches sprawled across a hillside. On registering at the reception, we were given a map with which to find our pitch. No problem. Tent set up, we rode back down the hill in search of some food in town. By the time we'd returned to the campsite it was dark. I fancied a beer, so we locked the tandem up outside the shop. I bought a couple of bottles, but on leaving the shop we couldn't find the key for the lock. Tom volunteered to run up to the tent and get the spare key, while I tried to work out where the original key had got to. Tom walked up the hill but after 15 or so minutes realised that he hadn't a clue where the tent was. In the meantime, though, I'd found the key in the grass by the bike. I decided to head up the hill to the tent, which, of course, I couldn't find either. Meanwhile Tom had returned to the shop to find me and the tandem... Thirty minutes of worry for both of us before we bumped into each other on the hill. Some teamwork and we soon located the tent. Relieved, we enjoyed a laugh about our predicament while sharing a bottle of beer.

After the talk I told Tom how impressed I was with his storytelling. I asked if he was nervous, to which he replied: "Yes a bit, but really it's just talking about riding bikes and I can do that."

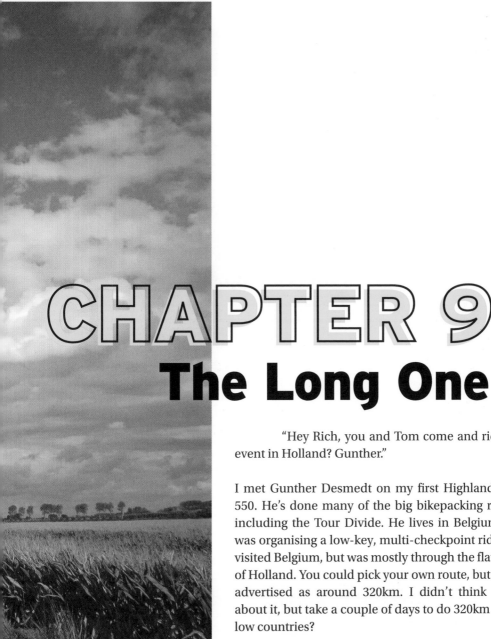

CHAPTER 9
The Long One

"Hey Rich, you and Tom come and ride my event in Holland? Gunther."

I met Gunther Desmedt on my first Highland Trail 550. He's done many of the big bikepacking routes, including the Tour Divide. He lives in Belgium and was organising a low-key, multi-checkpoint ride that visited Belgium, but was mostly through the flatlands of Holland. You could pick your own route, but it was advertised as around 320km. I didn't think much about it, but take a couple of days to do 320km in the low countries?

"Yes, sure, Gunther."

We were party to a Facebook group on the ride, but as I rarely translated the discourse that was mostly in Dutch or Flemish this may have contributed to having no idea as to which route to take up till a few days before the event. After a bit of begging, someone kindly emailed us a GPX file for us to follow with our GPS.

Tom borrowed a gravel bike from Alpkit for the ride. This was the same bike he'd used on his first 200km earlier that year. Quite why he opted to ride a gravel bike with gravel tyres on a 99% road ride I don't know, but it does indicate our level of 'planning'.

We drove to Dover after school on Friday and caught the evening ferry. We grabbed a few hours' sleep in the car near the start.

At 8am we congregated at the appointed place and chatted with friends from at least four countries we'd met on previous bike rides. What quickly became apparent was that everyone else here knew that the ride was to be completed inside a day. Two hundred miles on a bike in one day? Let's just consider that for a moment. In my 40-plus years riding bikes I'd never ridden that far before. A year ago Tom hadn't ridden 100 miles in a single ride. Unknown territory. We were surely doomed. Although, as the route was a series of loops, it meant it would be reasonably easy to escape if we ran out of energy, and we were there anyway, so we decided to make the most of the day.

Gunther said 'go' and, with no real knowledge as to exactly where we were supposed to be going, we set off. Some people went one way and some the complete opposite. We followed the purple line on the GPS screen and probably set off a bit too quickly trying to keep up with some other riders. It didn't take long, however, before they started to take slightly different routes. Occasionally at one of the checkpoints we'd meet another rider, but as we left it would be in separate directions. Very confusing. We soon realised we were going to be spending the rest of the day alone and settled into a steady sustainable pace.

Despite our lack of preparation and having no real idea where we were going, Tom and I enjoyed the riding very much. Firstly there were no hills, unlike home where every ride has to have at least a few thousand feet of climbing. We'd occasionally head into a pretty town or village to visit a checkpoint, but for the most part we were riding in countryside. It was October, the sun still had some warmth, and the wind – which can be a challenge in those parts – was non-existent. There were, however, plenty of windmills and the route was never far from the sea or big rivers.

We had to get an elevator in and out of a tunnel to pass under the River Schelde as we made our way through Antwerp. Later on, by the coast at the mouth of the river, we had to take a ferry from Breskens to Vlissingen.

This was all very different to our usual riding. Posting a picture to Instagram of each checkpoint was proof of our passage. This was fine during the day, but once night fell it was more of an issue. With GPS recording our progress, that would have to do if evidence was needed. During the day we kept up a respectable 15mph average speed, which I calculated meant we'd finish in approximately 14 hours if we didn't stop, and we'd had longer days than that before. But as darkness fell near Yerseke, it became clear that we'd be out a while longer when I made a navigational error.

Somewhere around 14 hours into the ride, my mind must have wandered off. Around 30 minutes after visiting the checkpoint at Goes, Tom said: "We've been here before." On checking the GPS I realised he was right – we'd ridden seven miles in the wrong direction! Which, of course, meant that we had to ride another seven miles back to the route. Who needs to make a 200-mile ride another 14 miles longer? We certainly didn't. But being negative in such situations just makes things worse; we've learned it's much better to just laugh it off, which we did.

With about 25 miles left to go to the car, Tom was getting really tired. This was the only part of the route where was no shortcutting the distance as it was almost a straight line.

We'd no tent or sleeping bag, so stopping to sleep was not really viable, though I did have an emergency survival bag. I kept chatting, asking him random things he'd have to think about to try to keep him awake, which worked for a while. But only for a while... As we rode through the village of Nieuwekerk in the early hours of the morning, he could no longer fend off the sleepmonsters. Momentarily asleep, he veered slightly and crashed into a privet hedge. Some late-night revellers on their way home made the obvious assessment of the situation, commenting: "Father, your son has crashed." But Tom's relatively soft landing left him unscathed, and the shock of crashing kept him awake awhile before I resumed my incessant 'talking rubbish' tactic for the rest of the ride.

Just after 4am, some 20 hours after departing, we got back to Woensdrecht. I messaged Gunther to say we'd finished. Job done. We locked the bikes outside the car and got in our sleeping bags inside the car. We had four hours sleep before heading back to the ferry and our drive north in time for school and work on Monday morning.

That was a landmark ride for both of us as it's the first time that we've ridden more than 200 miles. Looking back, we definitely both pushed the boundaries of what we thought was possible in a day. Our final total was 215 miles. Had we realised that the ride was to be done in 24 hours we'd not have turned up. While we find it funny to remember the time Tom fell asleep on his bike, it's obviously not something we'd like to replicate and I no longer underestimate just how much sleep he really needs. Maybe sometime Tom will try to ride further in a day, but I don't think as a pair we'll be aiming to better that distance. I can recommend the riding in Holland if you don't like hills, though – over the 215 miles we climbed a grand total of 650 feet!

CHAPTER 10
Joining the Dots

Ever since I first completed the Highland Trail in 2014, Tom has shown an interest in the route. He'd been heard to say, jokingly: "If my Dad can ride it, it can't be that tough." The reality, though, is that this is a hard ride. We tried in 2015, but were thwarted by wet and windy conditions. At Easter 2017 we had another go, but the weather was too wintry for our lightweight set-up, and we bailed after only two days.

In the book *Joining the Dots* by well-known Scottish bikepacker and bike-riding advocate Lee Craigie about her Highland Trail experience, Tom said he was aiming to be the youngest rider at 12 years old so we were committed to do this sooner rather than later. With a reasonable weather forecast, we booked train tickets to Tyndrum for a third attempt. It would mean a week out of school, but you'll learn more in a week on the Highland Trail than you will in a classroom so we were cool with that.

In Tyndrum the night before we set off we bumped into Dave and Jamie, some local friends, in the pub. They were also planning to set off on the route the following day. Their goal was similar to ours – to get round inside eight days in order to see the riders who were setting off in the Grand Depart at 9am on May 27th.

On day one we got up early and left Tyndrum at 5.40am with the sun shining and the trails fairly dry. We were on familiar territory and the first few miles passed by quickly. At Loch Ericht, Dave and Jamie caught up with us, chatted for a bit, then rode on. We presumed it would be the last we'd see of them as they were obviously riding faster than us.

Tom and I enjoyed the empty trails. We were relaxed because our previous experience on the route gave us a certain amount of confidence. At Culra bothy we stopped for a sit down and a bite to eat. We were already making up time on our previous rides on the route.

Our plan was to get to at least Melgarve at the foot of the Corrieyairack Pass, as we had on our previous two attempts, or even Blackburn on the other side of the Corrieyairack. We arrived at Melgarve at 7pm. We both felt good, and decided to head on up and over the pass but first we needed food. We'd been eating lots of sweet stuff, so Tom suggested eating some of the cheese we'd brought.

I asked: "How much do you want?"

"Half each," said Tom.

So that'll be about 250 grams of cheese each then.

Nearing the zigzags on the pass I was overcome by a wave of tiredness and nausea. I quickly realised that the cause was eating a big chunk of cheese just before climbing up a steep hill. Tom was feeling grim too. A few moments later all his cheese and other sundry food items were delivered to the trail by his feet. He was careful not to spew on his shoes, of course. A couple of sips of water, and we were again heading up the hill. He's been sick before at a 24-hour race, so he knew the nausea would soon pass.

Once over the Corrieyairack we rolled down the hill to Blackburn bothy. Just before we arrived there we saw Dave and Jamie who'd already put up their tents. They were quite surprised we'd ridden as far as they had. Once in the bothy we lit the fire and ate a couple of our favourite dehydrated meals, which were just what we needed after a long day. Ninety miles done was a good start.

We awoke reasonably early on day two, and it was raining. After a posh pork and beans dehydrated meal for breakfast we descended to Fort Augustus. We spied Dave and Jamie's bikes outside a hotel where they were having breakfast. We stopped for a pot of tea and a chat before continuing north. Jamie said he was amazed at how strong Tom was. Tom says 'thanks' and grabs a slice of Jamie's toast.

As the day progressed, the wet conditions took their toll on my brake pads. An oversight meant that I'd not brought spares. I knew that Square Wheels in Strathpeffer was just off the route, but it would be a challenge to get there before closing time. At 5.20pm my phone finally had network connection so Tom told me what type of pads we needed and I phoned the bike shop to check they had them in stock. I let them know we might be a couple of minutes after closing time and we raced from Orrin Dam to Strathpeffer. Getting a full set of pads each and a couple of spares, we stocked up on food and then rejoined the route. The plan was to replace the pads at Oykel Bridge the following day.

We rode until dusk and, despite having to camp with the midges in a forest, had a good night's sleep. The sun greeting us as we packed away the tent next morning made a good start to the day.

By mid-morning we passed the place we'd stopped at the end of day three, two years before, so we were doing well and we got to Oykel Bridge nicely in time for lunch, which was excellent.

After eating, we just needed to fit the new pads before heading into the northern loop. Tom removed the old pads, and then realised the pads we bought were not the right ones. He's very good on bike specs, so this was an unusual mistake and we had six pairs of brake pads that didn't fit either bike. As his bike had more pads left than mine he'd possibly be OK, but mine were just about down to the metal. The nearest bike shop in our direction of travel was hundreds of miles away. It was looking like our Highland Trail aspirations were doomed again. I thought about the descents to come, and there were lots. We weren't giving up though and the brakes would have to last. It was not the first time I'd had bike issues up here. Into the northern loop we rode. With the odd shower of rain along the way, it was otherwise a lovely afternoon and on reaching Glen Golly we pitched our tent on a windy knoll to avoid the midges.

Day four began with a climb up through Glen Golly – first riding, and then pushing, setting the tone for the next few hours. The route takes on a different character up towards Bealach Horn. This is a land that has faint paths and few visitors. There's lots of hikeabike, both up and downhill. It's a tough section and it certainly intimidated me the first time I visited. Eventually we crested the hill to arrive at Bealach Horn.

We stopped to take pictures and enjoy the far-reaching views, feeling fortunate to be there. A place and a time that will always stay with us, not least because I am so proud of Tom's achievement in getting there.

But time was passing, so we were soon giving it beans on the descent towards Achfary where we got some food and discovered that my water bottle had ejected itself somewhere on the fast descent. From Achfary there's a stiff climb, which always seems to be tougher than it should although I revel in the fact that we'd turned the corner and were heading back towards the finish. After this climb is another quick descent, which took us south along the coast road to Drumbeg. We stopped for lots of food before heading on to Lochinver, where we arrived in pouring rain. Naturally, our shelter of choice is the 'Pie shop' where we could eat more food. Having missed the worst of the rain, we headed a few miles further to Suileag bothy and a roof over our heads for the night. We arrived to find a fellow traveller already in residence. I only mention him as he offered us a cup of tea which would have been normal hospitality, except for being cross when he asked if we had tea bags and we answered 'no'.

Day five and the 4.30am alarm got us up and away early, despite both yearning for more sleep. From the bothy we followed the Ledmore traverse through Glencanisp, which looks almost flat and innocuous on the map. Progress through the rocks and many boggy sections was slow, though on this occasion, not quite as slow a trudge as I remembered and, in fact, with our plus size tyres we rode quite a lot of it.

We got back to Oykel Bridge by 10am for bacon sandwiches and coffee before taking the mountain road to Ullapool where we had a fish sandwich. More food? Always a good idea!

Oh, and remember those brake pads? We bought a hacksaw to chop down the ones we bought in case we really needed them, though I was getting used to metal on metal braking by then.

After Ullapool comes the Coffin Road, a long, steep, grassy climb that just keeps on dishing out the pain. From the summit we rolled down to the Dundonnell valley. We'd made good progress, but as it was still relatively early we continued onward, heading for the climb over into Fisherfield, because Tom really wanted to get to Shenavall bothy for the night.

Just before the top of the climb Tom started feeling unwell – his breathing was suddenly tight and his cheeks worryingly flushed. I tried not to let on, but I was really worried. I felt we needed to retreat so I persuaded him that heading back down the hill for the night was the best option, though he wanted to carry on. I promised how he felt the following day would decide if we could carry on. A couple of hours later he was feeling better, by which time we were snugly tucked up in a bunkhouse back in the valley. The following morning I thought it was best that he had a lie-in, so the day didn't start too early. Tom said he was feeling fine, so after breakfast we retraced our route from the previous day and were soon looking into Fisherfield. It was good to see so little water in the wide river. With the crossing barely ankle-deep, Tom made his own way across while I took pictures.

The next eight miles took around four hours. Some riding, but lots of pushing and tough going for anyone with a loaded bike. And the day didn't stop giving.

After the Fisherfield crossing comes the Postman's Path – more pushing and lifting bikes over fallen trees, up and down steep-sided ravines. We stopped just short of Kinlochewe for the night having done a grand total of 30 miles, but whatever had upset Tom on the previous day had thankfully passed.

There comes a time on these trips where you think there's a good chance that you're going to make it, and with only 160 miles left to do in two days I could now visualise the end. After Kinlochewe we headed into the Coulin Forest towards Coire Lair, down to Strathcarron for ice cream and then a small climb over the hill to Dornie for a pub lunch in the warm afternoon. There's a cheeky road climb that avoids the main road and goes back into the wilds of Kintail.

Just past Glen Licht House, Tom shouted for me to stop. His front wheel was leaking sealant from one side and the middle of the rim. Time passed and the sealant wasn't sealing, but helpfully, it was only escaping slowly. A quick bit of thinking and I managed to slow the leak with the aid of some cable ties. Eventually the sealant blocked the hole, though I felt it might only be a temporary fix and couldn't help but think we would once again be thwarted a finish. The next section was pushing, followed by a fairly smooth descent – amazingly the wheel held. We rode on until dark and put up our tent in a dense cloud of midges.

Next morning had to be an early start if we were to achieve our goal of under eight days. A couple of big, lumpy, but rideable hills took us over to Fort Augustus for brunch and then we followed the Caledonian Canal down to Fort William. It was hot so we stopped at Corpach as Tom was yearning for ice cream – naturally we stocked up on other food too. From Fort William we followed the West Highland Way to Kinlochleven. Walkers on this normally busy route were scarce at that time of day. We fuelled our descent with a half a lemon drizzle cake each. As we started the climb up the Devil's Staircase, the last big climb of the Highland Trail, the sun was setting and by the time we descended the other side of the hill we needed our lights. It's fair to say we were both really tired on those last few miles back to Tyndrum. The temptation to sleep was great, but finishing in under eight days was far more important.

At 2.10am we arrived back in Tyndrum having ridden 101 miles and climbed over 9,000ft. Our total time was 7 days, 20 hours and 25 minutes. We were pleased and surprised to find that Alan Goldsmith and Mark, who'd had attempted an ITT but abandoned, had stayed up to see us in. My wife had instructed Alan to give Tom a hug at the finish and he nearly knocked Tom off his bike as he hugged him because he was so pleased to see him.

We went to bed about 3am, but got up early to see off the riders who were starting their Highland Trail 550 that morning. It was wonderful to see people taking time out of their last-minute preparations to shake Tom's hand, especially those who'd previously ridden the route. While they lined up at the start, Alan got a selfie with Tom and then Tom had the honour of setting the group off.

The following year Alan invited Tom to ride the Highland Trail with the Grand Depart riders. He also said that maybe he should ride self-supported, which meant carrying all his own equipment. Tom did, and once again finished the Highland Trail 550.

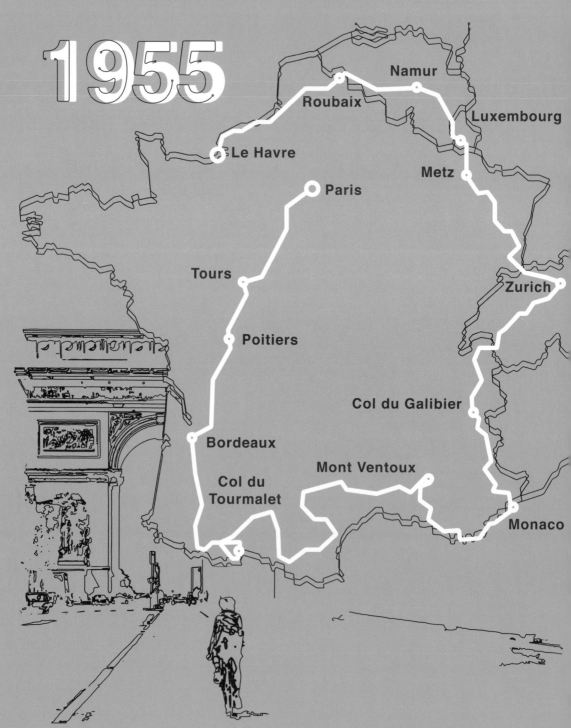

THE TOUR DE FRANCE
1955

Namur

Roubaix

Luxembourg

Le Havre

Metz

Paris

Tours

Zurich

Poitiers

Col du Galibier

Bordeaux

Mont Ventoux

Col du Tourmalet

Monaco

2950 MILES

CHAPTER 11
Rest or Race

If you ride a bike I'm sure you've been asked many questions, one of which might be 'Have you ridden the Tour de France?' I certainly have and Tom's also been asked several times if he'd like to do it. In the summer of 2017 we decided to loosely follow the route of the 1955 Tour. Over 34 days we rode 4,744km, climbing and descending 54,310m.

The route of the 1955 Tour was in a clockwise direction starting from Le Havre. Our 'Tour' visited each of the stage start and finish towns. At the start we matched the 1955 riders' daily mileage, but as the stages got longer and hillier we contented ourselves with just having a long day on the bike. By the time we made it to the foothills of the Alps via Belgium, Luxembourg, Switzerland and Germany, in retrospect, though there had been no dramas, we were weary. Maybe we'd pushed ourselves a bit too hard.

Day 11 dawned and we'd spent the previous night rough camping just outside Albertville – by the time we arrived at our planned campsite they'd already locked the gates. In our first 10 days we'd ridden 1,027 miles with the last day accounting for 118 miles, which included the 1,000m climb of the Col des Aravis. We were both tired and ended up having to clear some shrubbery to get a place to put up the tent. When we woke that morning, Tom's face had some sort of rash on it in the shape of a 'Z', like the mark of Zorro from the TV programmes I loved as a kid in the '70s. I tried to be nonchalant, but I'd never seen anything like it.

I could see that Tom needed to see someone with medical knowledge. I suspected he'd had an allergic reaction to the shrubbery we'd cleared, so I grabbed a couple of leaves to take as a reference. We rode down the hill to Albertville to find a person with medical knowledge. Being ill in a foreign country is difficult I've found, even if you speak a bit of the language. While I have the vocabulary for ordering food, drink and a bed, explaining a malaise is tricky.

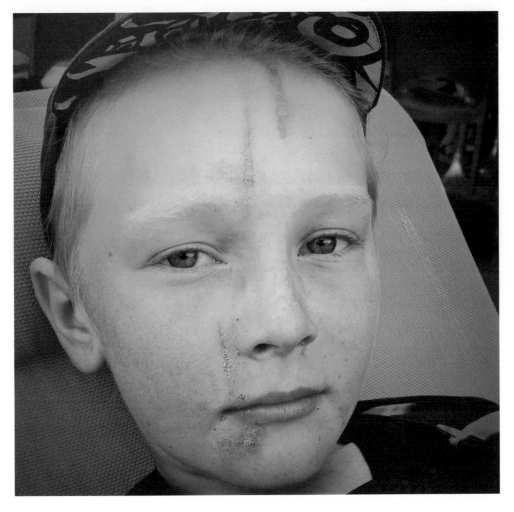

At the pharmacy I pointed to Tom's face and asked, in my best French, while waving leaves in my hand, why Tom might have been visited by Zorro while he was sleeping. In this kind of situation the person I'm speaking to would usually leave their mother tongue and speak perfect English instead. Not that day. Thankfully the pharmacist did know what the problem was. Through the medium of French and mime he explained that the UV had caused a cold sore (herpes simplex virus), which had quickly become virulent because of our exertions over the previous few days. He asked if we'd been using a high-factor sun cream. Embarrassed, I answered 'no'. We left the pharmacy with a large bottle of factor 50 and a small tube of 'repair cream' for night-time use, which I presume was made from the tears of a mythical creature as the two bottles came to nearly 50 euros. And I was told in no uncertain terms that Tom should have a few days' rest. A couple of days would be possible, but Tom wanted to keep riding although his face was itchy. I splashed factor 50 on him and agreed to keep on riding, but make it relatively easy. We'd been averaging over 100 miles a day so we'd just do 70, though there would be some hills.

We rode up the Col de Télégraphe early that afternoon. Tom was so much stronger that year, stronger than he'd ever been, and we played games on the way up the climb, toying with each other. Sprint. Catch my wheel. Drop me if you can. But, as always, we teased without any intent to really drop each other. After all, neither of us were pro racers – just father and son riding unsupported around the route of a Tour that had taken place ten years before I was born.

At the top of the climb I sat drinking Orangina and people watching; Tom had popped inside for a wee. It was a warm afternoon and crowded with people arriving by coach and car. I watched the steady stream of cyclists, many stopping to take a picture to commemorate their achievement. Stylish Europeans with their tanned skin and beautiful bikes were in the majority. One guy in particular caught my eye, not young, but giving it beans as he neared the top and, turning the final corner, looked back as the pros do. The look that said he was a winner. Bosh. When his friend turned up, they congratulated each other. Not a race, but a bit of friendly rivalry I guessed. A while later a couple more pals

joined them. From their kit and lack of suntan I guessed they were from the UK. An idle observation. Tom returned and I filled our water bottles ready to go. No more time to sit – we still had a way to ride.

We headed down the hill to Valloire. Hungry at the bottom, we shared a baguette filled with salami and cheese. Fuel to take us up the next climb, which was a big one. The Col du Galibier is a classic climb that has featured many times in the Tour. From Valloire to the summit is 18km – over that distance it rises 1,245m, with an average gradient of 7%. Early on in the climb many sections are less than 7%, which, you can guess, means there are some steeper bits nearer the top. The plan was to ride up to the top of the Galibier and camp up there for the night. It was around 5pm; we've eaten, it's cooled down, there's no rush and we're relaxed, so we made our way steadily out of town at a sustainable pace. I guess earlier in the day there would have been lots of people riding up and down, but it was quiet by then. Sometimes Tom was on my wheel, and sometimes alongside. We chatted for a while, then were quiet. No more sprinting for signs as we'd done earlier in the day.

I spotted a couple of riders coming up behind. The first rider didn't look at us as he rode past and he said nothing. The second guy, who was a bike length behind, grunted 'Bonjour' in Frenglish. I recall the guy who'd smashed it to the top of the Télégraphe and his mate who'd finished just behind him. I called out 'hi'. They returned my greeting, but weren't hanging about to chat. They weren't rude, but neither were they polite. The encounter irked me a little, but whatever. I could have let it go.

As the two riders edged away from us, Tom came alongside. He looked at me questioningly. No words spoken. I wiggled two fingers, gesturing Tom back onto my wheel. I lifted the pace very slowly. For maybe ten minutes we just held them at a static distance ahead. As they turned a corner they could see they weren't dropping us. Neither of them were smooth riders and I was making them uncomfortable by slightly raising the pace. They clearly didn't want us to catch them, though. I dropped to a slightly harder gear and Tom did the same. Slowly, in fact, very slowly, we accelerated. It took a while, but as we came alongside, I greeted them with a loud and cheery 'hi'. We let them hold our wheels for a couple of minutes, then it was time to push on. We tried to make our acceleration imperceptible. Tom could sense what I was doing and he stayed glued to my rear wheel. As we turned round another of the zigzags we could see we'd opened up a bit of a lead. I felt strong.

A flick of the wrist and Tom came alongside, smiling. He passed me and dropped another sprocket. Apparently he felt strong too. It would have been cold if we were riding at touring pace, but we weren't. We were sweating and, though not gasping for air, we were both breathing fast, taking turns through and off like racers do. I warned Tom not to go too hard. As we made our way up we could see the two riders were having issues, now a long way back. I moved to the front and held our pace, occasionally pushing on a bit to see if Tom could stay with me. Indeed he could. I had to stop myself going too hard because Tom was matching my every move and I was worried he'd overstretch himself. With six bends left to the summit, Tom dropped one gear and then another. He was out of his saddle and jumping on the pedals as if he was racing an unladen bike to the summit top finish of a Tour stage. I had done my part as his domestique and was happy for him to take the stage victory alone. When I crested the summit I was spent. Tom was smiling.

After the Alpine passes came Mont Ventoux followed by the Pyrenees. More mountains and more of the country we had both come to love.

Following the Pyrenees we rolled through the French countryside to Paris where, just like in the Tour de France, we finished on the Champs-Élysées.

It was great to see Tom so strong at the age of 12. Until that day on the Galibier I'd always been the stronger rider, but had known the tables would be turned one day and Tom would be waiting for me on the hills or shielding me from the wind on the flat – we were so nearly at that point in time. Now I'd have to ensure I was on top of my game to keep up with him. I was confident at the end of this trip that we both had physically what was needed to have a really good go at the Tour Divide.

CHAPTER 12
Everesting

Rested up after our Tour de France trip, Tom and I looked for a late season challenge to put our fitness to use. Initially we'd planned to head up to the Lakes and do a big ride on our mountain bikes, the Lakeland 200 – a 200km mountain bike loop of the Lake District, but reports said the ground was very wet after recent rain. We'd tried it once before on the tandem and had a soaking, so we weren't keen to repeat that. We were after a plan B.

While round having supper with us, James (our friend who'd raised the idea of doing the Festive 500) mentioned that the previous week a 14-year-old had become the youngest to complete the Everesting challenge. A simple, if not easy, thing to do, to 'Everest' is to climb 8,848m of ascent on one hill in one ride. Pick any hill and ride as many repetitions as you need to take you over the height of Everest.

Impetuous curiosity had made me embark upon my first solo Everesting ride on the road to Mam Tor in England, close to where we live. Tom first attempted one on Holme Moss in England when he was ten years old. He climbed just over 5,000m before his knees started to complain on his under-geared bike. Undeterred and determined to return and finish the challenge, Tom fancied giving it another go. Everesting fitted our needs well. After all, nobody is getting younger.

We chatted with James about suitable hills that hadn't yet been Everested, and he suggested the gem that is the road to Stwlan Dam. A gem for a number of reasons. Firstly, it's a gated road so no motor vehicles except for access for dam maintenance. Secondly it's a fairly consistent 10% gradient. Finally, it is a really pretty place to ride a bike – the road has sweeping switchbacks just like the ones you will find on alpine passes. The weather forecast for the following weekend looked OK with less than 1mm of rain forecast, so we decided on a 2am Saturday start. James kindly offered to meet us down there and support our attempt.

Tom and I drove down on Friday evening and as we arrived just after 10pm it started raining. We reclined the car seats, and I set the alarm for 1.30am. The alarm went off, but I'd not slept as the rain had kept me awake. I messaged James, who had by then arrived and was sleeping in his car, to say that I'd reset the alarm for 6am. The alarm went off, I woke up and it was still raining, though with added hailstones. We are frustrated by the weather...

Lazily I rang James who told me the nearby Lakeside café opened at 9am. It was just after 7am; I could see the cloud starting to break and the rain was just showers. Tom woke up, didn't question the weather, and just started putting on his cycling gear. So I did likewise.

A couple of ascents of the hill before breakfast at the café had been the plan. Once we'd started there was no time for that proper café stop because the weather improved and we were committed to giving this a proper go. James, our sherpa for the day, went to the café to get us a sausage sandwich and a coffee.

The weather was a mix – one minute fine, the next we had our waterproofs on again, although, as the day progressed, the rain lessened.

After our tenth climb and nearly a third of the way there, we were both feeling great. All those cols in the Alps and Pyrenees on our Tour de France with laden bikes had made us strong.

James kept us fed and watered. We put in a request at the beginning of a repetition and by the end our sustenance was ready. As well as catering for us, James rode a good number of ascents with us.

By the time darkness had come, we'd done 20 ascents with only 14 left to do. We were well over halfway, though it certainly wasn't a done deal. We were both slowing down a little. Needless to say, as the night progressed, we both felt more and more tired, though our spirits were high. We talked all the time on the way up the hill. If you are talking to someone your focus is on the conversation, not the blister on your bottom, or the fact that you'd rather be tucked up in bed than pedalling your bike.

I noticed a mechanical as I was grinding uphill – I'd lost two of my five chainring bolts. Back at the car James quickly came up with a solution by pinching one of Tom's and checking and tightening all the others.

And, wow – a clear sky at night in rural Wales means the stars can put on a show and they certainly did. We'd stop for a few moments at the top of the climb and try to take some of that in.

The descents at night were cautious – there were lots of sheep on this hillside, many of which apparently like sleeping on the road. They'd move out of the way in good time as we climbed the hill, but by the time we'd turned round and started descending they'd be strewn all over the road again.

We were nearing our goal, but we were riding slower. It was getting colder so we tried to minimise stopping time at the car. We wanted this done inside 24 hours.

One last stop at the end of rep 33. We turned off our lights for the final time, grabbed a handful of Haribo sweets washed down with some Coke and headed back up the hill in the dawn light.

At the dam we hugged each other, then took a 'summit' picture with Tom holding his bike above his head. James was waiting back at base camp for us to take the obligatory finish line photo.

Tom Seipp aged 12 years 7 months 22 days, the youngest person to complete an #everesting – 8,954 metres climbed in 23 hours 21 minutes.

AUX
SOLDATS
FRANCAIS
1914-1918

CHAPTER 13
High Rouleurs

Buoyed up by Tom's efforts on the Highland Trail 550 in 2017 and 2018 and our 1955 Tour de France trip the previous year, I was pretty sure he'd manage the Tour Divide trip. Early in the year I started looking at costs, which were substantially more than I'd guessed. Flights plus living expenses would need saving up for. Looking back, there was definitely an element of trying to put off any possibility of failing on such a great undertaking. It was also easier to postpone for another year rather than splash the bills on a credit card. I wanted to give it our best shot. One thing that stuck with me though were some words from Col, one of the founders of Alpkit. "Do you think you'll still go and ride the Divide?" I guess he thought we'd changed our plans.

We were desperate to ride somewhere, even though we were focused on saving for next year. So where hadn't we been in the UK? We had about a week, so where could we go to get there and back home inside seven days? We looked at a map – as usual we both had ideas, but I suggested Pembroke as neither of us had been there before and Tom agreed. We used an online route planning tool to avoid busy roads to get us to St Davids. Quiet roads, canal paths, bridleways – this route had them all. We had a plan.

We were blessed with good weather as we left home on our first day of riding. Familiar streets soon gave way to unfamiliar roads. When we arrived in Crewe we decided that it was time for some lunch. We visited a local supermarket and ate our purchases in the supermarket car park. As we left England and entered Wales the hills became a bit hillier, but the riding was not difficult. Tom and I each carried our own equipment – a trial run for the Tour Divide so we'd have the ability to be independent of one another. As the light started to fade we neared Newtown in Powys and decided to get some hot food in town. We spied a kebab shop and ordered a chicken kebab and some cans of fizzy orange. We ate quickly as we were mindful that we could do with the remnants of daylight to find somewhere to wild camp on the other side of town. It didn't take us long to find a corner of a field in which to stealthily pitch our tents and we were soon asleep with the alarm set for 7am. One hundred and thirteen miles done.

The following morning we broke camp quickly as it was drizzling and we didn't want to get cold. We rode to Llanidloes to have our breakfast in a warm café, where we bumped into Phil who runs a mountain bike guiding company in Wales and who'd heard of our exploits online. The rain abated slightly as we left the café and we were soon climbing up into the hills. The next section was distinctly lumpy. At Pont-rhyd-y-groes we spied a café where the owner fed us the most delicious homemade pizza. As the day progressed the weather improved. We were having a great time for sure, but this trip felt too easy. We were visiting new places and doing reasonably long days, but we compared this trip with others and both decided it was like going on a holiday.

The following day we arrived in St Davids around midday. We found a campsite, pitched the tents, then holidayed the rest of the day. We went to the beach and ate fish and chips followed by ice cream and enjoyed the sunshine. In the evening we climbed to the high point near the campsite and watched the sun going down over the sea. The air soon cooled once the sun had set, so we jogged down the hill back to the tents.

The initial plan was to retrace our tracks to return home, but we decided that would be dull so we made a few diversions from the straight-line route we'd arrived by. The weather was gorgeous, so we stopped often to get a cold drink. We even managed to find a craft brewery where I sampled one of their beers. Leisurely we made our way back north. It was quite nice, though strange, to know that this trip was not a challenge, but just a ride to be enjoyed. There was no need for asceticism. It took three days to return from St Davids. We didn't rush and put no pressures on ourselves in terms of deadlines; we just enjoyed riding our bikes. A sort of recalibration of what our bike riding was all about. But niggling me was the feeling that we should have really been out on the Tour Divide and being challenged.

The niggle developed over the next few weeks of Tom's summer holiday with us both thinking that it would be good to do something tougher, something that would stretch us and remind us that we still had what it takes. After some thinking and discussion we hit on it. Back to Everesting. After Everesting the Stwlan Dam road in Wales, Tom told me that if we ever did another such ride it would have to be in a different country because I'd already ridden one in England and one in Wales. The seed of something was sown, though to be honest I wasn't in a big rush to do it again.

We were heading over to North France for a few days and because we'd be away with the girls, we were ok to disappear for about a day – Tom first suggested that we revisit the Paris Roubaix cobbles. The talk of cobbles moved over the border to the Belgian 'bergs. I told Tom about the Tour of Flanders cobbles I'd ridden, and Tom reminisced about the time we rode up the Kemmelberg on the tandem during our French Divide trip in 2016.

Tom joked that we could 'Everest' one of the 'bergs, which to be honest I thought was a crazy idea. Riding up any of these hills once would not be a problem for us, but Everesting one? Simon Warren of *100 Greatest Cycling Climbs* books fame, has also written *Hellingen* which lists 100 climbs in Belgium. We had a flick through the book and shortlisted five climbs to have a look at.

The overnight ferry to Dunkirk saw us arrive early, but with not a lot of sleep. The plan was to find a climb on day one, ride it on day two, and then on the third evening of our holiday meet up with some friends starting a bikepacking race near Antwerp and have a drink. The nearest climb to Dunkirk is the Kemmelberg, so that's where we went first. This is the highest hill in the West Flanders region and was an important vantage point during the First World War. The memorial at the top (The Angel) is dedicated to French soldiers who fell in the 1914–18 war. At the foot of the western cobbles is an ossuary containing the remains of 5,294 soldiers, only 57 of whom are named. A hill with history.

We arrived mid-morning and walked up from the east, passing the now empty Restaurant Belvedere on the way to The Angel. We walked over the top to the west. This side, although steeper in parts, looked to be a better option as the cobbles weren't as rough. After getting the tent set up at a nearby campsite, we went back to ride both sides. Our initial thoughts were confirmed. We had a plan.

Just before 8.30am the following day, we parked the car at the top of the hill. By 8.30am we were at the bottom of the hill, and the GPS commenced recording. From the junction where we started, the road rises gradually from a gradient of 6%. As it rises it becomes lined with trees and the gradient starts to steepen, though it's still tarmac. Then the gradient steepens further and the *pavé* [cobbles] begin and the gradient keeps climbing to over 22%. There is no easy line through the cobbles. The climb has to be done seated to keep traction between the rear tyres and the stones. On the descent we soon opted for a line on the dirt just to the left of the cobbles, which saved our hands from the pummelling. This was a whole new level of hard.

The Kemmelberg is not a busy place, but there are walkers, fellow cyclists and cars to avoid at times. The plan was ride to five climbs and then stop, mark the lap sheet at the car and eat some food.

Late in the afternoon we were greeted by Pascal, an Instagram follower from Lille, who rode a lap with us before bidding us good luck for the rest of our ride. A short time later, while we were grabbing something from the car, the endurance rider Kristof Allegaert rode up. He'd heard what we were doing and had ridden over to see us, bringing Twix bars and Tom's favourite Coke. It was good to hear him tell us about the time he completed his double Everest ride. Apparently, it wasn't even planned – he just kept on riding after he finished the first one. Inspiring stuff.

As the daylight dwindled, so did the number of people. We were alone. Then, on lap 67, our friend Gunther turned up at the top of the climb. He'd also ridden over to greet us. He rode a lap with us, we chatted a bit and then he rode home. A little later one of the local residents came out with a bottle of Coke for us.

"How many times are you riding up and down our hill?" he asked:

I answered '137' and he told us that someone once rode 79 circuits of the hill. I asked why 79?

"That's all he could do," he shrugged.

Around climb 85 it came – the thing we dread on these rides – the lust for sleep. We nearly collided on the way up, a moment's inattention or maybe one of us fell asleep. We stopped, ate and drank more Coke to try to shake the sleepmonsters. We shivered uncontrollably as we rode back down the hill in the cold night air. Even though we were past halfway, I was unsure if we'd get to the end. Tom was tired and, unusually, I was tired too. We were both grumpy. We sat in the car for rests more often than we should have done, setting the alarm for five minutes on repeat, to make sure we didn't fall asleep. We both wanted morning to arrive. Salvation would come with daylight. Barely awake, we just had to keep turning the pedals. It was the longest night on a bike ever for both of us. Then dawn came and, like magic, the wish to sleep left us.

About six in the morning, Alan Goldsmith, Mike Toyne and Steve Heading called by to cheer us on – they were en route to a bikepacking race near Antwerp. Not long after that, the guy who'd brought us out a drink the night before made us some coffee and waffles. Twenty-seven hours in and we were back up to speed.

What was really cool in the morning was that Kristof turned up again with more snacks, drinks and encouragement. It was great he'd called by not once, but twice! What a star. We were hundreds of miles from home and yet we had so many friends call by. All people we'd met through riding our bikes. It was really amazing.

Then Ann and Skye arrived with drinks, pastries and sandwiches for breakfast, They stayed to count down the final ten climbs with us, which we savoured in sunshine.

One hundred and thirty-seven ascents of the Kemmelberg in one ride. Another Everesting done.

Postscript... I use a type of GPS which needs a computer, cables and an internet connection to upload long rides like these. So I didn't get to upload this ride until we were back in the UK four days after we'd finished. There was always a little niggle at the back of my mind that we'd maybe not completed the full 8,848m. Not exactly sleepless nights territory, but you get the idea. When I uploaded the ride, I found to my surprise that we'd climbed a total of 10,034m. The 'oversight' was caused by me referencing a segment on Strava on my phone that was nine metres shorter than the actual climb. What do they say about poor planning?

But every cloud has a silver lining... climbing over 10,000 metres in a ride admits you to the High Rouleurs Club, which is brought to you by the same people who created the sufficiently bonkers Everesting challenge. Tom was very happy! He's currently the youngest Everesting and High Rouleurs rider.

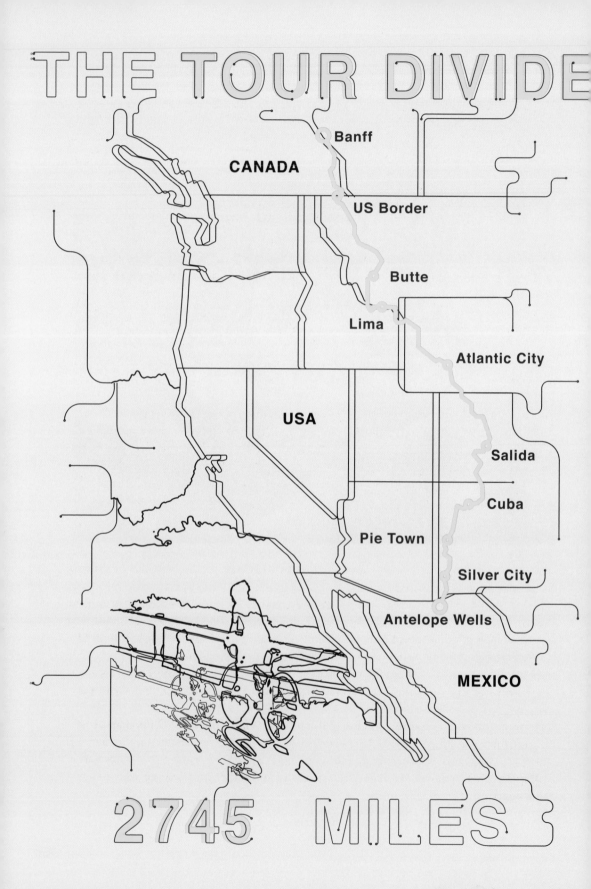

CHAPTER 14
No Surrender

Three words: The Tour Divide. Words that most mountain bike riders of a certain age will have heard of. A route that takes a rider from Banff in Canada to the Mexican border following the line of the Continental Divide. A distance of around 2,745 miles, which will also involve 150,000 feet of ascent. A route first ridden by the Moe brothers in 1984. A ride that many will dream of completing, but few will embark upon and fewer still will finish. I've known of it for many years, and several friends have ridden it. Realistically though, once Ann and I had kids, the likelihood of disappearing to North America for a ride that would take around a month was unlikely.

As Tom became a more accomplished rider, I thought maybe at some stage we'd be able to do it together. Alpkit had built the tandem which we intended to ride on the Divide when Tom was 11, but other opportunities closer to home took precedence, and by the time we'd decided that 2019 had to be the year, he'd outgrown it. The date was set for Tom's school holidays in July. It's easy to say in January that you have a plan when the end of July in Banff is in both senses a long way away. But I knew Tom wanted to be the youngest rider to complete the route, so there would be no more excuses.

I'm sure you'd now like to read about the hours of training that we did to prepare for this big ride. However, other than a week in Northern France and Belgium bikepacking as a shakedown ride for the bikes, we didn't do that much. Riders usually focus on a solid base of fitness – I've read you need to do the same miles in the preceding six months as you'll ride on the route. We'd done nearly 1,000 miles altogether and less than 100 in the preceding month, so I guess we weren't over-trained. I regularly asked Tom if he still wanted to ride the Divide and he always replied with a definite 'yes', but he didn't seem very enthusiastic about it as he'd been before. I'd never made him ride his bike and I certainly wasn't going to start, even though some bike fitness would have been useful.

One month before departure, I booked the tickets. Within hours I'd slipped and badly twisted my ankle. The following day the bruising was a purple and yellow sock halfway up my leg. Very painful. I was mortified by what I'd done and was definitely not capable of riding. On the bright side there was still a month until we left, and now a genuine excuse as to why we weren't out training.

I spent a small fortune on 'essentials' for our trip. We planned to ride unsupported, and needed two of everything because we wouldn't share any kit. 'Unsupported' means that you individually carry everything needed, and outside help other than what is commercially available to everyone is disallowed. This meant we both needed a full set of individual kit rather than sharing anything. The week before leaving was a mix of last-minute sorting out and worrying about what was to come. Turning up at the start of the Divide is the first step towards Antelope Wells, but so much could get in the way of an arrival at the Mexican border. Success rates are around 30%, based on those who leave at the Grand Depart. It would be too easy to enter a wormhole of all the things that could go wrong and not actually turn up in Banff.

In no particular order, here are some things worth worrying about. Bears. The route spends a lot of time in bear country. There are black bears and there are grizzly bears. The grizzlies are the bigger of the two varieties, but either will mess you up in a temporary or permanent way if you cross their paths and they are that way inclined. We bought a can of bear spray each and made sure we knew how to use it. Next up: thunderstorms. More than one person has embarked on the route and been hit by lightning. One of the earliest accounts I read of someone riding the Divide referred to the terrors of being in the middle of nowhere. Agoraphobia. Culture shock. Homesickness. Not forgetting the classic 'we speak the same language, so we'll be fine'. For us we'd be a long way from home and psychologically that can have a negative effect on resilience. Then, of course, there are problems of a physical nature. Overuse injuries, saddle sores and respiratory issues... and the damn bike breaking down on you. Two to four weeks depending on your ride speed leaves plenty of opportunity for any of the above.

The morning of our departure dawned and I only wanted to ask Tom one question, one which I'd asked many times before.

"Tom, are you sure you want to do this ride? I don't mind if you don't, but this is the last time I'm asking you."

His reply?

"Yes, 100% yes."

We threw the boxed bikes in the back of the car and Ann took us to the airport. We queued nervously to check in. Instead of paying for bikes, I'd paid for two boxes that weight-wise were within our hold luggage allowance. We got away with it. We said our goodbyes to Ann, gave her hugs and kisses and hoped we'd see her again in five weeks' time... not a flippant comment – in 2010 David Blumenthal was killed by a truck while riding the route. But as soon as we were on the first plane, any worries I'd had in the past were set aside. This was it, the big one. Tom and I were going to ride the Tour Divide.

Our Facebook pal Ricky and his partner Sue picked us up at the airport in Calgary and kindly drove us to the campground in Banff. The first one I've been to that comes complete with roaming elk. We were clearly no longer on familiar ground. There was no time to give our surroundings much thought though, as our priority was to reassemble the bikes and head into town to get supper before an early night. The next day we went for a short ride to find the beginning of the trail, which would be one less thing to do the following morning. We also did last-minute shopping that included those cans of bear spray. In the evening we ate pizza and decided we'd aim to roll out of Banff at 9am the next day.

Up at 6.30am, we packed our bikes and rode into Banff to find the ubiquitous Maccy D's for breakfast. The ordering system had a useful calorie counter, so we did our best to maximise our energy intake. Some young guys who were going to tour some of the route kindly took a picture of us before we headed to the start. There was no ceremony as we left the trailhead – no one to see us off; we just got on our bikes and headed down the trail.

The first few days we were mostly surrounded by trees, but every now and then there would be a glimpse of big mountains that still carried some winter snow. The fine weather on that first day soon turned wet and windy – this might be summer, but the weather could throw anything at us. And we saw our first bear, which happily decided that running away from us was a sensible course of action.

Over the next few days we settled into a rhythm following the mantra: 'ride, eat, sleep, repeat'. Our previous experiences on multi-day trips ensured we didn't try to go out too fast, or try to achieve big mile days too early. Instead we focused on looking after ourselves so that we'd be good to do it all the next day. We'd been asked how long we'd take and guessed at 25 days. Very early on it became clear that our days would have to get longer as our fitness increased if we were to come close to that, but having a total of 35 days in which to complete the ride, there was no pressure.

We rode through Canada and got as far as Butte in Montana without too much drama. I took a picture of Tom in the diner there where we had brunch – he was dirty, but looked so happy. By the afternoon, things had changed. He'd been riding a little way in front of me when he suddenly stopped, dumped his bike on the ground and started to unlace his shoes. I asked him what was up.

"I'm done with this. My feet hurt, my hands hurt, and I am tired and I am fed up with this boring ride."

I quickly tried to parry each thing that was bothering him, suggesting solutions to his discomforts. For the first time ever Tom was saying he didn't want to finish a ride. I was shocked and confused. I explained, selfishly, that while he might want to throw in the towel, I wanted us to finish what we'd started. I said that being in the middle of nowhere meant he'd have to get back on his bike to ride out of there. I also said that pulling out of something like this should not be done when he was tired, reminding him that if he made it to the end, he'd have achieved something that few have, and he'd never have to come back and do it again. He agreed to ride on a while longer and see what the next day would bring. I decided we'd have an early night and a lie-in so he could recover a little.

The next day dawned and the usual sparkle in Tom's eyes had returned. We had camped near the top of Fleecer Ridge – this has a reputation for its very steep descent that some say is unrideable. Telling Tom that something might be unrideable will elicit one response. In fact, if you care to look on Strava for the fastest time down Fleecer Ridge you'll find his name on the top of it. Tom's mojo was back.

Three hundred miles later we had made it through Montana. One thousand miles ridden, over a third of a way to the Mexican border. Statistically, if you make it to the border at Idaho, you will finish your ride in Antelope Wells. All we had to do was keep riding.

After Tom's blip in motivation and commitment to finishing the Divide, in some way I felt extra pressure. Aged 53, suffering from saddle sores and aching knees that took it in turns to hurt me most, I'd been thinking of myself as the weak link for the last couple of years. I'd developed a bit of a cough, the sort of thing that if you were at home would stay for a couple of days and then clear up. Riding for 12 plus hours a day gives the body little time or resources to repair what would normally be a minor complaint. I tried to keep this to myself and tried to take it easy, but uncontrollable coughing prompted Tom to ask jokingly if I was dying. Even having revised our goal to 30 days meant we were still reliant on doing big days.

Riding towards the Great Basin I was finding it increasingly difficult to breathe after a coughing fit. Surely it would be better the following day? Off the bike I was OK, but as soon as I started riding I'd have to be careful not to breathe hard or I'd start coughing. That really annoying cough where an itchy throat creates a vicious circle – once you start, it won't stop. The reality was that I was not getting better, but worse. I've taken Skye to hospital a number of times when she was younger as she struggled for breath suffering from asthma. A responsible adult would take me to hospital, but I was determined we would finish this ride. A conflict of interest.

Would my body let me finish? Was I being foolish and putting my health at risk in chasing this goal? Maybe. I kept all this to myself. Tom was motivated again to ride to the finish, though he would have advised the sensible thing which would be to stop riding and go to a doctor – as would my family and friends who were following our trip. I kept on going. Tom and I had a deal, and I was doing my best to keep my end of it.

After struggling to breathe on the hills, it was good to find a stretch of flat. Not so good was the killer headwind which whipped up loads of dust. With the combination of wind and dust I was really struggling to breathe and also having dizzy spells. Definitely getting worse, not better. If I made it to Salida, the next town, without resorting to pressing the SOS button on our satellite tracker, I decided I would find a doctor. As we rolled down the hill into town we were greeted by two dotwatchers, Brian Steele and Jacqueline (Billy Rice's mum). Brian and Billy are Tour Divide vets; Billy had also done it on a tandem with his daughter Lina when she was 16 – one of the youngest riders.

My throat was so sore I struggled to speak, but managed to ask for help finding a doctor. The next morning we had a sleep-in. Tom liked that. Then we headed for the Medical Centre.

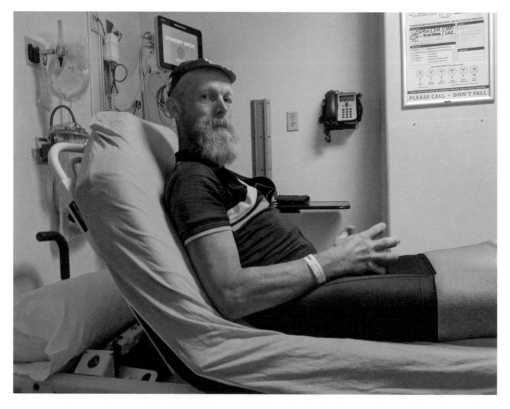

After various tests the doctor decided that I had pneumonitis and explained the most effective treatment was at least a week of rest. I explained that this was a less than ideal treatment as we were riding to the Mexican border. Cheerily he informed me that he was used to awkward patients, but he could prescribe some medicine that might aid my recovery. Twenty minutes on a machine inhaling salbutamol followed by being handed a course of tablets and an inhaler and I was good to go. Though I was happy the diagnosis wasn't anything more serious, he said if I wasn't better within five days I must find another doctor.

We left Salida sometime after midday, heading in the direction of Marshall Pass – one of the big climbs of the Divide. The wind was in our faces again so we were pleased to see somewhere to stop for a drink, though only a few miles out of town. We stopped at the Elevation Brewery in Poncha Springs where we relaxed and enjoyed the company of the staff and customers and, yes, we had a few drinks. I was beyond relieved that we could continue our ride, and the urgency about making sure we made it to Antelope Wells in time to get a flight home was waning. That evening we made it over Marshall Pass and onto Sargents – just a half-day's riding, but definitely a day of progress. Thankfully, over the next few days, the tablets worked and my cough gradually cleared up. We did just enough miles to make sure we'd get finished in time to get the plane home.

And then we were nearly there. One hundred and twenty five miles to go. We rode into Silver City rich in many ways, but not in food or water. The last couple of days had been borderline for sustenance. We were tired, thirsty and hungry. The afternoon weather forecast looked dodgy, but that was fine. All I wanted to do for the rest of the day was eat. By 1pm we had a hotel room and directions to a restaurant downtown. The food was good. Tom was adamant that tomorrow we'd ride the remaining 125 miles in one day, and, of course, if Tom's up for it, so am I.

We had the laziest start to the day though and arrived in Hachita, 45 miles from the end of the route, around 5pm. Geoff who owns a store there told us that Jeffery Sharp, who runs a Divide taxi service, was on his way to see us. We drank coffee and Coke and chatted to Geoff, who's had a go at riding the Divide. We also chatted with the border police who asked if we were going to ride to the border that night. I'm all for swerving a late night, but Tom says we'll be fine. They warned us about illegals.

Lightning to the right of us and lightning to the left as we headed south. Snakes on the road too. My lights kept on cutting out. We managed with just Tom's. We were tired, but so very happy. There was nothing that could have stopped us that evening. Every now and then Tom would grab my attention and we'd fist pump like the cool kids or hold each other's hands like the old people do.

We rolled up to the border gates around 10pm, 32 days after leaving Banff. A lovely warm evening with no one else around. I took some pictures and then we waited for our lift back to Hachita. We waited a good while, but it didn't seem long enough considering the time it had taken to get there.

I've seen so many pictures of people standing in front of that border sign over the years. You won't look at them and say 'wow, that's a great photo', but it's a thing of beauty if you've just ridden 2,745 miles from Banff to stand by the sign.

At the Mexican border, for that moment, we were both completely content.

FINALE

I've seen it written that the Tour Divide changes you. Though I do my best to avoid life's clichés, finishing the Divide has changed both Tom and me. It asks a lot of a person, both physically and mentally. It also takes a period of time to recover from those efforts and to process them.

I look back on the Divide as being the boss level of a complex video game that we had finally both completed. Each level from Tom's first ride at the age of five being a little harder than the one before. In the film that Dom Bush made about him, Tom, then aged 11, said: "If you can ride 5 miles, you can ride 50 – you just need to try a little harder." Ride 50, 100, 200 miles. Ride up hills. Ride across countries, round countries, climb the equivalent of Everest. Seek out the hard rides. Twenty-four hours on a bike. Two thousand, seven hundred and forty-five miles along the Continental Divide. All levels completed.

Our bikes stayed in their boxes for a while after we got back from the US. We'd both dug deep to finish the route, and though the bikes most certainly weren't to blame we were in no rush to get back on them again. Tom had to go back to school and explain those weird tan lines and I went back to work. Normal life sort of resumed. How do you process riding 2,745 miles on a bike in a month? If you ask me how was my ride yesterday or how was dinner, I could quickly give an answer. Neither of us had an immediate answer to 'how was the Divide?', other than how much tougher it was than we had thought it would be.

We did some organised talks a couple of months after our return, and as we told our stories and showed our pictures I hoped there would come a catchy little phrase that would sum it all up. There wasn't one. We told the truth and it didn't fit into a black or white catchphrase. There was definitely a sense that we'd achieved something, yet with a side order of negativity.

We had a date in October that we'd signed up for pre-Divide. Some unfinished business – a 130-mile ride in Belgium. We had failed the year before in some grim weather. The ride was dispatched in a clinical way without the usual pleasure, but instead with a sense that a box needed to be ticked. Riding bikes was supposed to be fun? We'd maybe lost that somewhere along the route of the Tour Divide.

December came and a brief discussion as to whether we would ride the Festive 500, which we'd completed six times before. The answer was 'no'. I wasn't bothered and neither was Tom. It seemed that maybe it was time to turn off the games console.

Tom spent time learning the guitar and keyboard and just watching YouTube. I started writing the book you're reading. I'd occasionally suggest that we go out for a ride, and very occasionally Tom would say yes. We'd not moved apart, but Tom just didn't want to spend as much time on the bike. We had rare moments capturing the feelings we'd had in our halcyon days, but things had moved on. Tom could go out on his bike on his own now without my guidance. Many years ago one of my friends Budge had said: "Cherish your time with your kids, as one day they'll be grown up and they'll be doing their own thing." For the first time in ten years I got used to riding my bike on my own again.

We are still often asked 'what's next?'. In our community there is a pressure to go even further or faster all the time, but is it healthy to be constantly striving for the next big thing? Tom and I are both content. We've visited some great places and made some great friends along the way. Oh, and we've had a whole load of fun, which was always the intended outcome of riding bikes together.

So what does the future hold for me and Tom riding our bikes together?

Well, the good news is that, after the impasse following the Tour Divide combined with the restrictions of pandemic lockdown, the band got back together for a ride up north to Cape Wrath this summer. We rode some trails we'd ridden before, along with some new ones. There were no deadlines, no 'set in stone' routes – we were just free to have fun on bikes once again. I think that's something we've missed for a while now.

There are a couple of other pencilled-in event entries for the rest of the year and even next year, but we have an eraser to hand if things don't suit. Tom and I both have some 'solo' ideas for rides over the next few years too. Tom will be 16 next year.

Would we do it all again? Absolutely. We are both fortunate to have spent so much time together learning things along the way. We've had true adventures, the outcomes of which have sometimes not turned out the way we would have hoped.

We've adapted, grown stronger, and learned from our mistakes.

If I can give one bit of advice as a parent? Spend time doing adventurous stuff with your kids.

September, 2020

ACKNOWLEDGEMENTS

As Tom once said "I've not prepared an emotional speech," but I do have a number of people to thank for their contributions to our story.

Thanks first to my wife and daughter who have had to put up with Tom and me disappearing for weeks at a time and all the bike bits that litter our house.

Steve Bate who kindly accepted my request to write the foreword for the book.

Photographers who allowed me to include their pictures in the book: Dom Bush, James Lyon, Simon Barnes and Mark Armitage.

My daughter Skye who designed the maps for the book.

The organisers like Gunther Desmedt who have allowed and encouraged Tom to take part in their events, but especially Alan Goldsmith and the Strathpuffer team.

All our Kickstarter friends for their generous support.

Finally a big thanks to Heather, Jo and Rhiannon who've shuffled my ramblings and pictures into the book you have in front of you.

BIOGRAPHY

Richard Seipp lives in the Peak District with his wife and their two children.

He is a lifelong cyclist, and over the years has tried most facets of the sport. Never at the front of the field, though a competitor in many races, including Megavalanche, the Three Peaks Cyclo-Cross, and many 24-hour mountain bike events.

Happiest being outdoors with family or friends.

Blogs occasionally on **www.thecyclerider.com**
Tweets and Instagrams more often at **@richpips**.

KICKSTARTER
Thank You

Alan Trought

Alanna and Robyn Smith

Allen Boardman

Andreas Braukmann

Andrew Tonkin

Andy Acourt

Andy Howard

Andy Peretti

Ben Kerridge

Beth and Badger

Brian Steele

Budge

Callum Sword

Carl Hutchings

Chris Bees

Claire Brook

Daisy Knowles

Dale Bird

Daniel Jones

Deborah Rose

Fraser and Kate

Gairy Mannion

Gav, Sal, Joe and Archie Stretch

Gilford D Sweetenham

Greg Cummins

Hannah and Norna

Harald Legner

Harriet

Hippy

Iain Jagger

Ian Fitz

J. Thurber

James Lyon

Jamie Bell

Jane and Julian Winstanley

Jason (Ride Holme) Budd

Jim Dockal

Joan Carrillo Olesti

Joe France

John Vincent

Jon Wyatt

Jonathan Humphrey

Jules Jordan

Kerrie Thornton

Les Telford

Martin C.

Martin Hickman

Megan Ellen Wilson

Mel and Shaggy Ross

Michael Donnelly

Michael O'Connell

Mick Riley

Neil Cottam

Neil Fettes

Neil Pirie

Nick, Zoe and Sam Wallace

Owen Smith

Paul

Paul Griffiths

Paul Nutton

Pete Winkley

Phil Nightingale

Phill Millward

Pieterjan Heyse

Pyro

Rich McPhaden

Richard Grieve

Richard Moss

Richard Wilson

Rob Bob Penny

Rob Walker

Robert Armour

Ruben Casier

Ryan O'Reilly / Victory Chimp

Sam Orridge

Simon and Susie Race

Spencer Long

Steve, Ann, Jemma and Ged Waters

Stuart Miller

The Kelly Family

Theakston00

Tim Ruck

Tomo

Toon Timmers

William Foley

Wiz Lees